LIVERPOOL
GHOSTS and GHOULS

RICHARD WHITTINGTON-EGAN

THE GALLERY PRESS
LEIGHTON ROAD, NESTON, SOUTH WIRRAL

ISBN 0 900389 24 9
Published by Gallery Press 1986
© Richard Whittington-Egan
Printed by Leemancolour Ltd., Neston, South Wirral.

The Liverpool Dossier Series
All titles in this series were originally published in Richard
Whittington-Egan's earlier books, LIVERPOOL COLONNADE
and LIVERPOOL ROUNDABOUT.

Now available:—

Back in the days when the Beatles would still pop into Ye Cracke in Rice Street to take a friendly ale with me, I was paying a young man's court to the fickle jade of the Mersey. I wrote two love chronicles of our on-off affair—*Liverpool Colonnade* and *Liverpool Roundabout*. Oh, I was a knight-errant then, pricking in fancy my milk-white palfrey through the stone forest and down the avenues of my imagination. And such imaginings! I saw the Liver birds take wing against a low lying hunter's moon . . . the chimney-masted tangle of sky-riding roof-tops looking at dusk like the decks of ships at swaying anchor . . . I heard the golden and porcelained names on windows singing the old crafts' songs and lullabies of trade . . . I lurked around the Western bazaar counters in the lit grottoes of the shops . . . I rode the overhead railway and the Noah's Ark tramcars . . . watched the glittering city slip over the horizon's edge into the purple pomp of night—and out again into the watered-milk light of another dawn. Both I and the Liverpool of which I wrote have grown up, grown different. We have played weather-vanes to the wind of change. And yet we are still the same at heart. The fresh wind blowing across the river and over my city's wild hilltop still whispers the old tales to those who are willing to listen . . . a light still burns in Paradise Street. . .

CONTENTS

1. WONDERS AND HORRORS IN LIME STREET

"The Chamber of Horrors used to be in this cellar," said my guide as he led me down a precarious flight of steps into the bowels of Lime Street.

Upstairs, the pipes and drums of a ceilidhe, which was in progress on the top floor, mingled their swirling music with the staccato clicking of balls on the billiard-tables which now occupy the other two floors of what was once Reynolds's famous Liverpool Waxworks.

"Of course everything has completely changed since old Reynolds's time," explained my companion in a voice which many years of life in Liverpool had not robbed of its granite-edged Scots accent, "the building has been practically gutted. Only the entrance hall and walls are as they used to be. As for the rest . . . you would think it had been stirred with a stick."

Looking around the bare, whitewashed basement it was difficult to realize that once upon a time thousands of people had paid their eager sixpences to feast upon the horrors which were the quondam tenantry of its arched recesses. Now, there was nothing more fearsome than the huge furnace crouched like a slumbering monster in the corner. Almost apologetically my guide said that it was rather dull nowadays, but his eyes lit up as he recalled that one day in 1922 he had stumbled upon a very fine cast of Charlie Pearce's head, gruesomely divorced from any suggestion of a body, rolling in the rubble.

It was round about the year 1860 that Alfred John Reynolds, the Tussaud of the provinces, decided to settle down in Liverpool. He came from his native Bristol via Birmingham, Leeds, Bradford and Manchester, and he brought his travelling waxworks with him. Looking about for a permanent home for his exhibition, his fancy lighted upon the old Freemasons' Hall in Lime Street. Here, he first established a dining-room and then, a year or two later, installed his effigies for what was to prove a stay of sixty years.

The new waxworks was a tremendous success from the start and perhaps its greatest attraction was that grisly section in the basement—why are such things always situated belowstairs?—which Reynolds dubbed "The Criminal Chamber." Here were to be seen the waxen shades of most of the criminally illustrious of their day, and Charlie Pearce was prime favourite in an unholy company which included such notables as Franz Müller the first railway murderer, Palmer the Rugeley poisoner, Mrs. Dyer the baby farmer and Mary Eleanour Pearcy the perambulator murderess.

The catalogue of the Criminal Chamber is an enchanting document written in the lost language of an age which combined relish for salty details with a tone of high moralising. Thus, of William Dove, executed at York in 1856 for the speeding of his spouse into happier realms with the aid of a liberal libation of strychnine, it says: "His parents were examples of kindness and humanity and gave their son a liberal education, having had him brought up at the College near Leeds; but Nature, which baffles the calculations of man, formed him of a cruel disposition. . ."

Not far from Dover stood the stiff likeness of Captain Henry Rogers, "A jolly master (by repute), who systematically murdered members of his crew in the days when ships were sunk for the insurance money." This merry mariner was eventually hanged in grim old Kirkdale Gaol for the murder of Andrew Rose, a seaman aboard the *Martha and Jane.*

Reynolds always displayed a proper pride in this criminal gallery of his and spared neither effort nor expense to do the right thing by his public. Anxious to secure a model of James Berry, the master-hangman, he did not hesitate to pay that worthy craftsman the sum of £100 for sittings. During these sessions Mr. Hangman Berry whiled away the time with cosy little tales of the platform manners of various clients who he had "turned off." At the time of Mrs. Maybrick's arrest in 1889, Reynolds was very keen to prepare a model of the accused in readiness to fill a place of honour should she be convicted. Unfortunately for him, before the trial began Mrs. Maybrick's mother—the Baroness de Roque—flitted frantically around buying up all the existing photographs of her daughter. Not to be thwarted, the single-minded Reynolds betook himself, sketch-book-in-hand, to the court and with the aid of drawings which he made of the woman in the dock constructed a very lifelike waxwork. Despite the subsequent offer of many hundreds of pounds from Mrs. Maybrick's affronted relatives, the wily old proprietor steadfastly refused to remove the offending effigy from his exhibition.

Upstairs, where the shaded lamps made the tops of the billiard-tables look like so many smooth, green islands in the dusky sea of gloom which surrounded them, I stood in what had once been part of the Great Hall and my mind reached back to a February night practically seventy years ago. That night had been an historic one, for it had marked the 25th anniversary of the opening of his Liverpool Waxworks, and Alfred Reynolds had celebrated with a grand banquet. At 11 p.m. precisely, some 300 guests had sat down at tables laid out in the centre of that vast hall of waxworks and there, watched by the glassy eyes of the silent dummies which crowded the shadows, they ate and drank beneath the brightly-flaring gas-lamps. An observer might be forgiven for thinking that sorcery was abroad that February evening, for, shifting his gaze from the still effigy of the Prince

8

of Wales to the seat of honour at the main table, his astonished eyes would have discovered the Royal original occupying that place. The Master of Ceremonies called for silence and Mr. Reynolds rose and proposed the health of the Queen. Glasses were lifted and the Grand Orchestrion pealed forth the National Anthem. His Royal Highness responded for Her Majesty and the Grand Self-Acting Organ obliged with "God Bless the Prince of Wales." Prince von Bismarck raised his glass to "the prosperity of the institution," the Chairman made graceful acknowledgement and the Beautiful Automaton Pianiste rendered a sparkling fantasia on one of Erard's Grand Pianofortes.

★　★　★　★

That glittering banquet represented the zenith of Reynolds's Waxworks. From then on it is a sad story of gradual decline. In 1913 the Waxworks hit the headlines again, but this time it was with a report of a social occasion of somewhat inferior calibre. Some burglars who had raided the adjoining warehouse of Messrs. Rylands had dropped into the Reynolds's via a skylight and, having helped themselves to the contents of the refreshment bar, had descended to enjoy a picnic among their peers in the basement. Bottles of pop and cakes, with Crippen as guest of honour, were the highlight of their achievement.

During the years that followed various attempts were made to renew a waning public interest in the Gallery of Illustration by the importation of a number of freaks. There were the Orissa twins, Craio the missing link and the lion-headed boy: but the old Waxworks was dying, being strangled it was said by a new-fangled invention—animated pictures.

In the past the theatres had provided a certain competition but this had been successfully countered by the production of a series of pantomimes, *Blue Beard, Robinson Crusoe, Sinbad the Sailor* and the like, with marionettes as actors and actresses. Moving pictures, however, proved a more formidable foe. There was a final desperate flirtation with the enemy. A bioscope was installed and gave two shows daily. But it was all of no avail and in 1922 the auctioneer's hammer fell and finally shattered Reynolds's Waxworks.

Among the lots listed in the sale catalogue were some intriguing items— a model of Little Tich which danced and bowed; an English execution with brand-new clockwork; Ayella, a beautifully modelled female figure of a snake-charmer in handsome oriental dress with snakes and alligators and electric fittings for lighting up the snakes' eyes. There was also a bioscope and, representing perhaps the last concession to a conquering enemy, "Charlie Chaplin performing the splits with pretty movement of a bird in a tree."

9

2.   THE DEVIL IN BOOTLE

Close to where, until German bombs razed it to the ground, the Church of St. Alexander lifted its proud spire to the Bootle sky, there is a very ordinary little cul-de-sac called Ariel Street. In this quiet, indistinguished street, there is a commonplace brick terrace house—Number 15—which, during the latter part of the last century, was the scene of certain occurrences so strange that they were regarded as nothing less than visitations of the Devil. Their commencement dated to shortly after the arrival, in July 1882, of a new lodger—a Miss Teresa Helena Higginson.

To all outward appearances, there was nothing peculiar about the pale, shabbily-dressed little woman who, between the years 1879 and 1886, might frequently be seen in the streets of Bootle. She was a mistress at St. Alexander's Elementary School, and her life was, superficially at any rate, in no wise different from those of her three fellow-teachers with whom she had come to live at Number 15. But listen to what the Reverend Canon Alfred Snow, a Roman Catholic priest, a man of considerable intelligence and integrity, and the 39-year-old Teresa's spiritual adviser, had to say of her:

"I feel I should do wrong if I died without leaving behind me a declaration which I now make . . . by my intimate knowledge of her, her interior, her way of life, her heroic sufferings, her trials, her writings, the analogy, between her life and the lives of the saints, all combined with my knowledge of mystical theology, of which I made a close study . . . I feel it right to say that I have a firm conviction that Teresa was not only a saint, but also one of the greatest saints. . ."

Nor was the Canon alone in this judgment, for, since her death in 1905, many people have come to a like conclusion and the Roman Catholic Church itself was at one time considering the question of her beatification.

Born on may 27th, 1844 at Holywell in Wales, whither her parents had gone on pilgrimage to St. Winefride's Well, Teresa's childhood was spent mainly as a boarder in the Convent School of the Sisters of Mercy at Nottingham, and from her earliest years she was remarkable for an amazing piety and charity of disposition.

In 1865, after an education frequently interrupted by illness, she left the Convent of Our Lady of Mercy and returned to her parents' home at Newton-le-Willows. A short time after her homecoming, disaster fell upon the Higginson Family, for some dealings which her father had had in the cotton trade failed owing to the American War and Robert Higginson went bankrupt. So Teresa and her sisters were obliged to go out and earn their own livings. One of them, Louisa, entered the Training College in connection with the Convent of Notre Dame, Mount Pleasant, Liverpool, to learn to be a teacher; another, Frances, gave music lessons, and Teresa herself, a first-class needlewoman, tramped the shops in search of orders for sewing.

It was in 1871 that by a seeming accident Teresa was thrust into the career that she was to follow for the rest of her life. In that year a terrible outbreak of smallpox ravaged the western counties of England. Liverpool was badly hit and one of the most severely affected areas was Bootle. Such, indeed, was the state of affairs there that many of the schools had to be closed down for lack of teachers. The Reverend Edward Powell, then rector of St Alexander's, much distressed by the threatened closure of the school which he ran in connection with his church, went to see Sister Mary Philip, the Mother Superior of the Mount Pleasant Training College, and begged her to help him. Unfortunately, she had at the time no qualified, or even experienced, teacher available, but she recommended Teresa Higginson, the sister of her pupil Louisa, who had, said Sister Mary Philip, a wonderful way with children.

So, for a few months, Teresa went to work at St. Alexander's School and when the emergency was over she decided, on Father Powell's advice, to take up teaching as a profession. Accordingly, she sat for her examination at Mount Pleasant, was sent to the Orrell School, near Wigan, where she gained her parchment, and, in 1873, was appointed headmistress of St. Mary's Infants' School, Wigan.

Here, she was soon joined by another teacher, Miss Susan Ryland, who was to become her closest friend and to whom we are indebted for the first accounts of some very extraordinary events. Susan and Teresa lived together in very close contact, sharing a single room and even sleeping in the same bed. Presently, Susan began to notice certain things about her companion which puzzled her. Often she would find Teresa in a curious state of unconsciousness. On one occasion she became so alarmed that, thinking her friend must be dying, Susan ran in terror for a priest. Upon his arrival, all he did was sprinkle the prostrate woman with holy water, whereupon she immediately regained her senses. Gradually, Susan came to realize that these sudden lapses into unconsciousness were not, as she had at first feared, the result of illness, but something akin to trances—Teresa was in ecstasy. She noticed, too, that the trances became more and more frequent during Lent, until, as Holy Week approached, she would lie for hours like one dead. On Good Friday, 1875, Teresa was found lying senseless, her arms outstretched, her body in the form of a cross, and with wounds through her hands and feet from which the blood oozed. There were also other and exceedingly unnerving manifestations. Fearful shrieks and yells would fill the house, the very walls would tremble to the sound of crashes like thunder and strange lights would flicker round the room. To the terrified Susan, Teresa used to say: "It is only the devil, dear. He just wants to be noticed, but he cannot really harm us. Let us say our prayers." Sometimes there came a loud knocking on the door and when Teresa opened it she would receive a violent blow in the face from an unseen hand and would stagger back with her cheek all red and swollen.

After three years of this sort of thing, Teresa's health began to give way and she returned home to rest. In 1877, however, the Jesuits opened a small school in the village of Sabden, near Clitheroe, and Teresa took charge of it. She stayed there until 1879 when Father Powell offered her a post in that same St. Alexander's School where, eight years before, she had first heard the call to teach.

The seven years which Teresa was to spend in Bootle were to be the stormiest of her whole life.

She went first to lodge with a Mrs. Nicholson, who kept a small shop next door to St. Alexander's Church. Here, she remained happily for about three years. There is evidence that the trances and the terrible agonies of Holy Week continued to take place throughout this time. Indeed, Mrs. Nicholson's little daughter, Helen, afterwards admitted that she had distinctly seen the stigmata wound on one of Teresa's hands, but the Nicholsons did not go about talking of the weird experiences of their lodger and she was left in peace with her secrets. Teresa occupied the back bedroom nearest to the church and it was sitting at a table in the window, from which she could clearly see the red gleam of the brightly-burning sanctuary lamp, that she wrote, at the direction of her confessor, a series of wonderful letters—the autobiography of a soul, one might call them—in which she displayed a knowledge and understanding of mystical theology which astounded the good priest to whom they were addressed.

In July 1882, Mrs. Nicholson died and, at the invitation of three of her fellow-teachers, Terresa moved into a Mrs. Flynn's house at Number 15 Ariel Street where they all lodged. One of these young teachers was a Miss Minnie Catterall. She is now dead, but she has left an exceptionally vivid account of some of the fantastic occurrences in that secluded little house. "She had not lived long with us," writes Miss Catterall, "when I was very much alarmed and frightened. My sister and I occupied the double bedroom next to that occupied by Miss Higginson. On a certain night we had just retired to bed and extinguished the light, when I was terrified by a terrific noise on the landing and walls which I could never describe. . . As far as I can remember the same thing happened the following night but even worse than before, which, of course, made me quite distressed as no one else in the house heard anything." This went on for some time until one night, "there was a more dreadful noise than ever, as if the walls of the house were being banged together, and this time it was heard by everyone. We were told by Father Powell that the noises were made by the devil, but not to be afraid, as he could not possibly harm us. On another occasion I heard him walking with a tremendous foot on the landing and wriggling the handle of the door most dreadfully; and again, as if someone, suspended over the door of Teresa's room, was laughing and screeching with the most hideous and fiendish laugh. . . I had just settled myself one particular night, when suddenly I felt the warm breath of a huge crawling beast coming stealthily towards my hand with its tongue and large teeth."

It is hardly surprising that with things of this kind going on people began to talk. In accordance with Teresa's wishes, her friends did all they could to suppress the rumours which inevitably leaked out, but it was not long before she found herself the centre of a storm of controversy. Those who knew her, either praised and revered her as a good holy woman, or else denounced her as a liar and a hypocrite and said that the noises were caused by "the devil coming to claim his own." Tongues wagged, folk claimed that they had caught the smell of strong drink upon her breath and seen her reeling drunkenly about the streets. She was accused of making prayer an excuse for neglecting her school duties and, time and again, as the frail little woman struggled down the road with a huge wooden pail of steaming soup for the poor in either hand, her detractors would mock and shout "Old humbug!" as she went quietly by on her errand of mercy.

Eventually, the situation got so tense that Father Powell was removed from the parish and six months later his successor dismissed Teresa from the school.

She still had nineteen years of life left to her. Twelve of these were spent in retirement in St. Catherine's Convent, Edinburgh. In July 1899, her family, who were then living in Neston, wrote to Teresa and asked her if she would come and help them, as her sister Fanny was very ill and required a great deal of attention. After Fanny's recovery, Teresa was approached by Canon Snow who told her that one of his teachers, a Miss Maggie Garnett, was in great difficulty owing to the illness of her sister, and suggested that she might go and help. Eager, as ever, to be of service to others, Teresa joined the Garnett's in their home above the little shop which they kept at the top of Mount Pleasant and there she remained tending the invalid till her death in 1903.

By now, the time of Teresa's own death was rapidly approaching. On November 23rd, 1903, she received a letter from the Principal of the Mount Pleasant Training College offering her a position as village schoolmistress at an obscure cottage school at Chudleigh in Devon. She arrived at that desolate spot in pouring rain one early January day in 1904. It was as she was preparing to come home to Neston for the Christmas holidays, 1904, that she suddenly had a stroke. She was put to bed in the little cottage and a nurse was sent for to look after her. For a time it seemed that she was going to get better, but at ten minutes past eleven on the night of February

15th, 1905, she died. They took her body back to Neston on a winter's morning when the ground was white with snow, and buried her beside her mother.

Well, that is the strange story of the Devil in Bootle and the woman who fought him there and all her life: as curious a tale as you will find anywhere in the wonderful and variegated history of Liverpool. What you decide to make of it is up to you. If Teresa Higginson was a hypocrite and an evil woman, it is odd, to say the least, that she should have impressed practically all who came in contact with her as a most pious and saintly person; it is odd that Susan Ryland, the friend who she so influenced at Wigan, should afterwards have become a nun; it is odd that the nurse who attended her during her last illness should, shortly after Terresa's death, have become a Poor Clare, entering one of the strictest religious orders open to women; it is odd that, half a century after her death, she is remembered, and her memory venerated, by thousands of pious men and women the world over. Many of us find little difficulty in believing in such marvels as are said to have marked the life of Teresa Higginson, only providing that they happened in a sufficiently remote past, but when they occur to someone we could have known, someone who walked our city streets and whose eyes beheld the familiar Liverpool scene, we boggle at accepting them. And yet, why should not such things be? Is the God of the twentieth-century—or the Devil for that matter—any less powerful than the God of Abraham and the mediaeval saints?

3. GHOSTS OVER MERSEYSIDE

Faces that peer at you through a mist.

Cold hands that stroke your throat and pluck at your bedclothes.

Eerie footsteps that ring out in the still watches of the night.

The shadow form, half glimpsed, that glides through a winter dusk.

Ghosts!

"You may be an undigested bit of beef," apostrophised Scrooge, "a blot of mustard, a crumb of cheese, a fragment of underdone potato," but for all that Jacob Marley's ghost continued to confront him clanking his chains and wringing his shadowy hands.

There are many people who, like the old miser in Dickens's Christmas story, will glibly tell you that "There's more of gravy than of grave" about those apparitions which we call ghosts, an assertion which it is difficult to deny. By their very nature, ghosts are impossible entities to assess. You can't put them in test-tubes or under the microscope; dissection and material analysis are out of the question, and objective investigation is all too frequently hampered by clouds of witnesses. Nevertheless, the belief in ghosts is as old as man himself, and from the earliest times there have been uneasy whisperings of unbidden guests who have made the night hideous and of weird happenings and hauntings which, defying all attempts at natural explanation, have struck terror into the hearts of those who have encountered them.

Among the masses of ghost stories which have troubled the centuries, many are patently ridiculous, many more are to be accounted for in terms of ignorance, superstition, indigestion, over-heated imagination and plain delusion. But there are others which are not so easily explained away, they are too well attested and rest upon firm foundations of evidence supplied by scientific and critically-minded observers.

Of recent years, the ghost has been at something of a discount: the whilom phantoms which were the beckoning ones outside the nursery window seem to have been ousted by Martians and space-visitors who stem from another kind of fantasy. It is the flying-saucer now and not the broom-bestriding witch that flashes past the moon's pale face! But there are still certain seasons of the year—Christmas for instance—that flee the mind to inglenooks and snug Pickwickian nights, when the old-fashioned spectre comes into its own, the music carpet is unrolled and folk love to cluster in cosy horror round the spurting fire to tell tales of *things* that lurk in the shadows beyond the circle of its light.

It is in this mood of faintly sceptical nostalgia, that I have been turning back the pages of local history and going out into the streets and lanes to investigate the rich lore of ghosts over Merseyside.

One of the most singular cases which I have unearthed concerns a house situated in a central Liverpool district. It will, unfortunately, be necessary for me to refer to many of the scenes of ghostly disturbances in such vague terms, because a house which is reputed to be haunted is often difficult to let, so difficult in fact that no landlord will thank you for spreading the tale of its haunting abroad.

In the year 1934, a Mr. C. Collins, who at that time was the proprietor of a Brownlow Hill bookshop, had the misfortune to purchase the aforesaid apparently desirable residence in central Liverpool, and took with him to his new home a sizeable family consisting of his 78-year-old mother, his two grown-up daughters, a brother and sister and a couple of friends, Mr. Ben Griffiths and his sister, who were to lodge with the Collins's.

"We spent a good deal on the house in one way and another," lamented Mr. Collins later, "I wish we had saved ourselves the trouble now, for we could not live there any longer after what we have gone through." It was to Mr. Ben Griffiths that there came the first indication that the house was a troubled one. His was a room on the top floor, and on the very first night he spent in it his rest was disturbed by a continuous subdued whispering which seemed to come from a trap-door in the ceiling. A little later he was alarmed by the sound of footsteps as though someone was "walking stealthily to and fro wearing dancing-pumps." The phenomena went on for about a week and were always accompanied by a cold little wind which blew across his bed. Then one night *something* began to pull very gently at his bedclothes. That was really too much. Voices and footsteps were one thing, but an invisible hand plucking at your blankets. . . He made up his mind to tell Mr. Collins the whole story. To his surprise, Collins confessed that he too had heard footsteps and felt the cold breeze. They agreed not to tell any of the others of their uncanny experiences for fear of frightening them, but now the occurrences began to become more unnerving. One night the shadowy form of a young man stepped out from a wardrobe door, walked towards the window and vanished. He appeared to be about eighteen or nineteen years of age and, moving in a kind of grey mist, threw a queer half-shadow on the wall. Once, when Mr. Griffiths was lying in bed, a face suddenly materialised close to his own and peered at him through a cloud of vapour. A crucifix hung at the head of Griffiths's bed, and he afterwards attributed his safety to its presence, for he heard a voice say in his ear one evening, "Only one thing stops me from getting at you." Mr. Collins's mother also had an alarming experience when, one night, she felt a small hand like that of a child stroking her throat. The climax came when Mr. Collins's daughter, Lily, arrived home very late from a dance. Her father was woken by loud cries of "Come quickly," and found the girl in a swoon outside his bedroom door. Trembling, she told him how upon her return

16

something had followed her up the dark stairway. Gaining her room, she had undressed quickly and jumped into bed. No sooner had she done so, than she heard footsteps in the room and when she called to her father they seemed to turn and come at her with a run. Then she felt a heavy weight as if someone had leapt on the bed. The family spent the remainder of the night downstairs huddled round the fire. The next day they left the house for good, and, said Mr. Collins, "Although I am a poor man, I wouldn't spend another night there for a hundred pounds."

By way of contrast with the foregoing authentic and apparently inexplicable—at any rate, unexplained—manifestations, I will now tell you of the farcical affair of the Ghost Pictures of Harrington Schools. It is a case which demonstrates very forcibly the power of mass hysteria and provides an object-lesson in just how careful one must be before assigning to any occurence, no matter how many people may vouch for its genuineness, a supernatural origin.

The first muted suggestion that something was amiss at the school premises in Stanhope Street came at mid-day on Monday, June 7th, 1926, when a young boy returned home for lunch with a breathless tale of having seen the likeness of a human face imprinted on the glass of one of the school-room windows overlooking Grafton Street.

Throughout the long sultry hours of that far-away June afternoon, the story of the phantom face was passed from ear to credulous ear. Women neglected their household chores to gossip on their steps and when, with lengthening shadows, evening fell and the menfolk came home from work, the tale was told all over again, embellished now and ornate with all manner of details and artistic refinements which had at first been lacking.

By now a drizzle of rain had begun to fall, but, nothing deterred, hundreds of people started to flock eagerly to Stanhope Street. The drizzle became a downpour, but still the crowds came to stand doggedly there in the rain just staring at the school windows. Suddenly an excited woman gave a loud cry: "There . . . look . . . on that window, the figure of Christ carrying the cross!" There was a buzz of excitement and men and women knelt down in the roadway and upon the rain-greased pavement.

As the evening wore on, the street became the scene of frenzied pilgrimage. Far into the night the people continued to come, a heterogenous collection of whites, negroes and Chinamen, who gazed reverently at what they were now calling the spirit pictures. A bluish smudge on one window was unhesitatingly identified as a thorn-crowned head and another became the Good Shepherd gathering His flock. An elderly woman who was still watching at midnight swore that a star appeared flickering in the centre of one of the panes of glass and that the colours of the pictures became as plain and clear as if it had been broad daylight.

17

In the small hours, a hastily summoned official of the school went round whitewashing a great many of the windows, but nevertheless when next morning the crowds gathered again it was not long before they had discovered upon another window a mirage effect which glistened in the sunshine and which was confidently hailed as the figure of the Virgin Mary standing in a rainbow.

By mid-morning, the congestion in the street had grown to such proportions as to have become something of a problem and the police were obliged to take a hand. Thereafter, each person was allowed a single glance and was then asked to "Move along, please."

Naturally, the pupils at the school became wildly excited when they saw the huge congregation in the roadway and lessons that day were carried on with considerable difficulty. Nor was it only the children's routine which suffered. The headmaster was besieged by a number of spiritualists and devout members of the public and, as he afterwards confessed, so impressed was he by the wonder and awe of the crowds that at one stage he had been loth to touch the windows, fearing that any such action on his part might be very fiercely resented.

Of course the headmaster himself was under no delusion as to the real nature of the marks on the windows which were the innocent cause of all the trouble. He said that when he had first come to the school he had noticed certain curious flaws in the window-panes. On investigation he found that the explanation was that the glass for many of these windows had been bought cheaply and had been previously used in shop-windows where it had been crusted with advertisements. The school window-cleaner confirmed that it was still possible to trace old lettering, vague eulogies of various brands of soap and chocolate, and said that in one sheet you could clearly see the imprint of a man's hand.

During the week immediately previous to that which saw the outbreak of the furore, the windows had been cleaned with paraffin, and it was the streaks of paraffin, together with the markings which were actually in the substance of the glass itself, which had been responsible for all the alleged phenomena.

In the course of the next night the remaining windows were duly treated with whitewash and the ghost pictures of Harrington Schools vanished like so many spectres at cock-crow. Indeed, you might say that the whole thing fizzled out like a damp squib in a window-cleaner's bucket.

But do not feel comfortably secure in the belief that all such occurrences end with satisfactory material explanations, for I will tell next of some Liverpool hauntings for which reason can supply no such adequate answer.

4. HAUNTED LIVERPOOL

In many unexpected parts of present-day Liverpool you will chance upon remote streets of fine old houses behind whose massive walls, which once formed the bastions beyond which were cradled the secure lives of merchant princes and other men of substance, there now live perhaps a dozen families who, like the houses that shelter them, have fallen victim to the economic rigours of this day and age. Such places resemble nothing so much as seedy museums, and that, in a way, is just what they are, for embalmed within the walls of the houses which form them are such memories as ghosts—if ghosts there be—must thrive on.

I know of one such house in which there is a room where a family of four have their being. It is a drab, gloomy apartment and its history is known to me. In that room a retired major, who doted too much upon the bottle, lived nightmare hours filled with those hideous things which emerge from too many empty bottles, and, shortly after the turn of the century, slit his throat from ear to ear. Is it too much to think that this incident, and others like it, may well have charged the atmosphere with something of the electric horror which accompanied its perpetration, or that unwholesome things might be attracted to sites where such frightful dramas have been enacted? Indeed, such theories seem tacitly confirmed by the fact that many hauntings, particularly historic ones, centre upon localities which are the scenes of past violence and brutality. Similarly, it has been postulated by those who devote their lives to the investigation of psychic phenomena, that the spirits of those who have "passed over" will sometimes return to places which hold memories of old happiness for them. Such ghosts are harmless, vaguely whimsical entities, and have been said to have manifested themselves in many parts of the British Isles.

It is to this class of phantom, I feel sure, that two spectres who paid a visit some years ago to a house in one of Liverpool's declining squares, belonged. The people who owned the house had gone abroad, leaving strict instructions with the servants that on no account were any strangers to be admitted during their absence as there were many valuables in the house. One day, shortly after their departure, a carriage and pair drew up at the front porch, a footman assisted a lady and a little boy to alight, and, as the lady rang the bell, the carriage drove rapidly away. When the maid answered the door, the lady asked permission to look over the house. Remembering her employers' instructions, the maid replied that she was afraid that would not be possible, whereupon the little boy burst into tears and his companion began to entreat her to reconsider her verdict, urging that she had vital reasons for wishing to view the interior. At last the housemaid gave way. Once inside, the stranger seemed thoroughly at home, running up and down the stairs and moving confidently from room to room without enquiry or hesitation. At length, stepping into a dressing-room adjoining one of the main bedrooms, she suddenly raised both her hands and, exclaiming in tones of the deepest gratitude, "God bless you for what you have done for me this day," she and the boy both vanished into thin air. The terrified housemaid searched the place from cellar to attic, the police were called in and they too combed the house, but with the same result, the mysterious visitors had completely disappeared and were never seen again.

Some years later, a visitant of a rather different kind plagued the peace of an old house in Sackville Street, Everton. Whatever it was, this intruder was decidedly malignant and its activities led directly to a woman being detained in hospital. The mystery began shortly after the woman, together with her family and those of two of her relatives, moved into the house. On the first night of their tenancy a house-warming party was arranged, and it was at about nine o'clock in the evening, when the fun and games were at their height, that one of the guests became alarmed by the sound of eerie footsteps moving about somewhere in the attic reaches. A search was made but revealed nothing to account for the noises. Unnerved, however, some of the women insisted upon the police being called. Three men left the first-floor room where the festivities were being held, to make their way to the local police-station. Barely had they gone, when a terrific crash brought the women, screaming with fright, to the top of the stairs. Below, in a dazed state, lay one of the men. He had been descending the stairs, he said, preceded by one of his companions and followed by the other, when he felt two hands grasp him round the waist, lift him as though he were a mere toy and send him gliding down the stairway. "I seemed to be wafted down," are the words he actually used. During the next three nights the house was filled with strange noises and the occupants were too scared to sleep. Eventually, they reached a unanimous decision to quit the place, and agreed to move all the furniture down to the ground-floor. The three men went upstairs to start on the job. One of the ladies followed them up and was nearly at the top of the first flight when she gave a piercing shriek. Her terrified relatives, rushing out into the hall, watched in open-eyed horror as they saw the woman float a few feet in the air, stay poised there for a second or two, and then come gliding down to where they stood fourteen feet below. According to their testimony, the woman kept her arms outstretched throughout her flight, her eyes were wide and staring and she seemed to be surrounded by a kind of halo of light. She dropped on her feet with her arms still extended and then shot through a doorway into a room. When the others followed her they found her unconscious and she was later taken to hospital suffering from multiple injuries and nervous shock. Just who or what it was in that house in Sackville Street that delighted in hurling people down the stairs was never discovered, but then no one knows what strange or horrible thing may have happened, far-away and long-ago, within its bland brick walls.

With its bright lights and constant traffic of pleasure, the Lime Street area is probably one of the last places in which you might expect to encounter a ghost, and yet a Mr. and Mrs. Cuthbert Wilkinson met two in a private hotel within easy walking distance of Lime Street Station. During the first night he spent there, Mr. Wilkinson awoke with a start and the impression that the echo of some loud noise was still ringing in his ears. Suddenly wide awake, he sat up in bed and saw in the moonlight which poured a cold stream through a nearby window, the figure of a tall girl in a light-coloured frock, apparently intent upon searching the pockets of his overcoat which was hanging behind the door. Thinking that she was a thief, Mr. Wilkinson promptly threw one of his shoes at her and to his dismay it passed right through the girl's body. She turned her head in his direction but seemed to be staring at something behind him. Uneasily, he looked round to see what she was gazing at so intently, but saw nothing. When he looked back to where the woman had been she had vanished. Instantly, he leapt out of bed and ran to the door. It was locked on the inside. Shaking violently, maybe because it was a cold night, maybe chilled by what was a most frightening experience, he scrambled hurriedly back into bed and pulled the blankets over his head. Later on in the course of their stay, Mrs. Wilkinson, too, was vouchsafed a ghostly glimpse. She was in the bedroom one evening preparing to go out. Crossing to the wardrobe to get her raincoat, she heard someone give a little cough behind her. Turning round, she saw facing her a very tall man in a bright check suit. He had dark, piercing eyes, black hair and a moustache, and she noticed that he held one arm in a sling. For a second or two he stood gazing straight into her face, then he walked to the window, which was wide open at the bottom, and leaned out. Recovering from her surprise, Mrs. Wilkinson ran from the room, but remained standing on the landing within full view of the door so that no one could leave by it without her seeing them, while a maid went for help. When the maid returned with the manager's wife and the hall-porter, they made a thorough search of Mrs. Wilkinson's room but found no trace of the mysterious intruder. The hotel in question has since been converted into offices.

Another one-time hotel—or rather lodging-house—situated in the heart of Liverpool's Sailor Town, and now converted into a garage, has boasted a ghost for at least sixty years. The phenomena follow a more or less standard pattern of footsteps, doors which will not remain closed and so forth. On several occasions the figure of a man dressed in the clothes of an old-time sailor has been seen, always in the same front room and always by the fireside. Again, one is not surprised by the advent of an apparition in such a locale for many of the old Liverpool seamen's lodging-houses were most

21

vicious places from which the shellback was lucky to escape with his life, let alone his money-belt.

Next, the black limelight switches to the spectres of suburbia, and I will recount how I spent a windswept night keeping a tryst with a phantom in plum-coloured trousers upon a desolate beach at Garston.

5. SPECTRES IN SUBURBIA

It was a wild churchyard night with the moon chasing the shadows, and anyone seeing our two figures upon the beach would have been hard put to explain why a couple of apparently sane men should be pacing the river-front at twelve o'clock on such a night. Had they questioned as and been told "We are here to keep a date with a ghost," they would most probably have revised their opinions concerning our sanity and have taken to their heels.

But there was no one there.

A savage wind tore at the clattering corrugated-iron fence of the bottle factory and drove stinging drops of rain into our faces. Over to the left stretched a barren dyke-rutted waste land, across which the flashing blue airfield location beacon of Speke Airport cast the periodic brilliance of its raking beam. In front of us, the murky-looking river and, looming stark and skeletal in the darkness, the battered hulk of a beached ship.

We had come to this forlorn fragment of foreshore because of a most unpleasant experience which had befallen my companion, Mr. William Routledge, who has a ship-breaking yard at this spot, one November night in 1951. At that time Mr. Routledge was engaged in breaking up a hundred-year-old, three masted, German barque called the *Fides*, and, anxious to fetch the vessel further in at high-water, which was due at 1 a.m., Routledge, his wife and his sister-in-law had piled into his car and driven down to the Garston waterfront at the bottom of Brunswick Street.

In view of what I am about to relate, I think it is only fair to tell you something about Bill Routledge himself. He is a big, greying man, an open-air type, who has done a lot of boxing in his youth and strikes you as a bluff, hearty sort of fellow with a strictly no-stuff-and-nonsense attitude to life. He is not by any means given to seeing visions and has been a lifelong teetotaller.

When, on that dark November night, Routledge and the two women reached the river end of the yard, they got out of the car and stood for some time looking at the *Fides* which was illuminated by the bright beams of the headlights. It was while they were standing thus, that Routledge's sister-in-law became aware of a slight movement on the waste ground on their left. She drew his attention to it, but, thinking that they had perhaps surprised a courting couple, Routledge tactfully told her to ignore it. A moment later, however, she was tugging at his sleeve again and, following her gaze, he saw an immense figure of a man rise out of the waste land. The man seemed to be of huge stature: "He looked at least six foot six," Mr. Routledge told me, "and I was particularly struck by his hair which stood up from his head in a great bush four or five inches high." There was

23

something about the creature's demeanour which Routledge found vaguely uncanny. At that moment, the thing began to advance towards them. Its gait was curiously stooped like that of a great ape. On and on it came, walking right across the yawning black gap of a dyke as if it were treading solid ground instead of the empty air. Then, as they watched, the figure passed right through the headlights of the car without breaking their beam, and disappeared before the corrugated-iron fence. Both Routledge and his sister-in-law saw the apparition, and noticed that his clothes were curiously old-fashioned, his breeches in particular impressed them as peculiar, for they were tight, tapering and plum-coloured. One of the most extraordinary, and in my opinion significant, features of the whole affair was the fact that while Routledge and his wife's sister saw exactly the same thing, Mrs. Routledge, who stood beside them throughout the manifestation, saw nothing at all.

On the night of our vigil conditions were, as I have indicated, certainly all that any self-respecting spectre could desire. We waited there for fully two hours, smoking our pipes and stamping our feet, as the keen wind cut through heavy coats which felt as if they were made of tissue-paper. But there was never a sign of the ghost. Once, an owl flew low over our heads with a loud screech which gave me a nasty turn, but that was all. Well, not quite all. It was shortly after half past twelve when I fancied that I could detect a very slight movement towards the edge of the waste land. I mentioned this to Routledge. "Where did you think that you saw it?" he asked. I pointed to a dark hollow some fifteen yards away from where we were standing. "Funny you should pick that spot," he said, "actually that is the precise place where I first saw the thing." It was odd, certainly, but hardly decisive, and although we watched for another thirty minutes nothing else happened. When, at last, we gave up the ghost, I came away with the impression that we had been on the brink of some strange experience, but I'm afraid I still felt intractably sceptical. Maybe I'm just not psychic.

Another waterfront phantom which is said to haunt the river-lip is that of Trash, the Ghost Dog of Formby shore, and there have been numerous accounts of its hair-raising activities. Otherwise known as "The Striker," because of the harsh, blood-chilling cries which some of the older folk claim to have heard it utter, and which, they will tell you, portend death or grave misfortune to those who hear them, this unpleasant ogre is said to prowl dark parts of the shore between Formby and Ainsdale. People who have met with it describe it as a gigantic, black hound with large luminous eyes. Local legend recounts how a man who lived near the coast and used often to return home at night very much the worse for drink, had the misfortune to encounter it upon one of these vinous occasions. Filled with fear and anger, he lashed at the dog with his stick, but the stick passed right through it and, fixing him with its eyes, the creature crouched down in front of him as if about to spring. The terror-stricken man fainted clean away, but when he recovered The Striker was still there, balefully staring at him. By this time the man had sobered up sufficiently to take to his heels and make a dash for it. Rumour cannot resist the moral corollary that the drunkard henceforth turned his back on the bottle and subsequently led a life blameless as that of the staunchest Alcoholic Anonymous!

Among the legions of spectres which have stalked the night-world of Liverpool's suburban dormitories, mention must be made of the Stoneycroft Horror which caused ten people to leave a house in that district. The story is told by Mrs. Birrell, a widow, who was one of the two people who actually saw the ghost. She was having a late supper with her daughter and son-in-law, Mr. and Mrs. Rex Harte, when one of the other tenants came and told them that weird creakings, groanings and footsteps were alarming the occupants of the ground-floor. Mrs. Birrell said that she would come down at once to investigate. As she was descending the stairs, there suddenly materialised in front of her a column of light which bore the vague shape of a human figure. The figure was completely transparent and after a second or so disappeared through the wall. Mrs. Birrell screamed and fainted, and at that precise moment all the lights flickered but, mercifully, did not go out. A few weeks prior to this harrowing experience, Mrs. Birrell had gone to the cellar to put some money in the gas-meter and something had brushed past her. She turned swiftly round only to find that she was the sole human thing in all that dim basement.

Rather more than a decade ago, the people of Prescot were worried by a ghost which was said to be flitting about the old stone-quarry by Delph Lane, Whiston. Whilst doing a spot of courting, a 24-year-old seaman had crashed a hundred feet to his death off an 18-inch ledge on the quarry-brink. Shortly after this tragedy, a woman who was returning from the last house at a local cinema was alarmed as she passed the pathway leading up to the quarry when she and her companion saw a man on the footpath. "There was a look about him that caused an eerie feeling to run down my spine, and when we got within half a dozen yards of him he disappeared," she afterwards explained. Crowds subsequently spent several nights "tracking" the ghost in the quarry, but nothing came of their efforts to lay it.

More recently, a ghost manifested itself in a house in Arundel Avenue, Sefton Park. The house was occupied by a doctor in those days, and his daughter told me that, being alone there at about four o'clock in the gloaming of a December afternoon, she heard the sound of a key being placed in the front door which opened and was then gently closed. Thinking it was her father returning early from his round, she called out, but received no answer. She went downstairs: there was no one there, but as she was ascending again to her room, she felt an ice-cold wind pass over her and, although she saw nothing, a palpable presence pushed past her on the staircase. I may say that the doctor's daughter is well-known to me personally and that I can vouch for the fact that she is not an imaginative type.

In the next chapter I shall be following the phantom footsteps across the Mersey—I almost wrote The Styx—into some weird byways of Wirral.

6. WEIRD HAPPENINGS IN WIRRAL

Rolling out the barrel is generally a hilarious process, unless, of course, it happens to be a ghost that is doing the rolling! In the present instance, the presence of a spirit outside instead of inside the barrel had a distinctly dampening effect on all concerned.

The house to which the following narrative refers is an old one situated in Birkenhead, and the floor of one of its attics is sullied with the dirty crimson flush of blood. This bloodstain is said to bear witness to a horrible murder which is alleged to have taken place in that attic many years before when the house was tenanted by priests. According to the legend, one of these priests was brutally killed there, and his corpse stuffed into a barrel, prior to its being secretly disposed of. A lady who subsequently lived in the house had many strange experiences there and came to the conclusion that there was a ghastly amount of truth in the tradition. Several times, just as the grandfather clock on the landing struck three, this lady and her two sisters were wakened by a thunderous knock. Intense silence followed, and then, from the very top of the house, there came a heavy rolling noise, horribly suggestive of the trundling of a barrel. Flight by flight, the thing bumped blindly down the stairs, pausing briefly at each landing, until the echoes of its bumpings grew fainter and fainter as it reached the cellar.

Another recently-revived story of a Wirral haunting tells of a phantom which flits through the premises of Oldershaw Grammar School at Wallasey. The ghost, according to Mr. James F. Ford of Cliff Road, Wallasey, who has recently retired after being a master at the school since it first opened way back in 1920, is that of Hubert Mayo, the school's first headmaster, who died in 1921. Mr. Alexander McGraw, now also retired after thirty-one years as art master at Oldershaw, is one of those who had an eerie experience there.

"There is one night at the school I shall never forget," he said, "although it happened all of thirty years ago." He had gone back to the school shortly after ten o'clock to frame some pictures which his pupils had painted, and did not leave the woodwork room until about half-past eleven at night. As he was closing the door behind him, he distinctly heard a rustle in the corridor like the swish of a master's gown. The passage was pitch-black, and when he got downstairs, Mr. McGraw stopped and listened, but all was still. It was a woman cleaner who actually saw the ghost one winter evening when she was filling ink-wells near Mr. Mayo's old study. The figure flitted past a room which had a stone balcony and to which there was no access. Terrified, she dropped a large ink-pot and fled in search of the caretaker who at once went round the school with a loaded revolver searching and locking all the rooms. He found no one.

Cutting across to the far side of the Wirral Peninsula, the serious ghost-seeker lights upon Thurstaston Hall, a magnificent old residence dating back to 1400, which is indisputably subject to periodic hauntings. The Thurstaston apparition is that of a woman who once owned the hall and was the last of her line to live there. She seems to have succeeded to its ownership by means of murder, for this woman confessed on her death-bed to having killed a little boy who was the real heir in order to secure the property for herself. Her guilt-seared shade manifested itself to a noted portrait-painter, Reginald Easton, who, on one occasion when the house was full, was put in the room where, more than a hundred years before, the murder was committed. He was told nothing of the ghost and retired to bed in all innocence. He awoke, however, in the small hours to find an elderly woman standing at the foot of his bed, wringing her hands and staring down at the floor as though searching for something. Not at first realizing that she was a phantom, Easton spoke to her, whereupon, after pulling the bell-rope, the woman vanished. The next day he told his host what had happened and heard the whole story of the murder. That night, Mr. Easton, who does not seem to have been afflicted with nerves, waited up for the old woman with his sketch-block by his side. She returned punctually, and continued to do so throughout the artist's stay. During her brief visits, Easton managed to complete a drawing of her, and when, afterwards, he showed it to one of her descendants, it was immediately recognised from the close resemblance it bore to a portrait of the murderess which had formerly hung in Thurstaston Hall but which had been removed thence three generations before and had never been seen by Mr. Easton.

Leasowe Castle is another ancient Wirral abode with a ghostly history. Formerly the residence of the Earls of Derby, the castle subsequently passed through the hands of many families. At one stage in its varied history, it came into the possession of a man who was involved in a bitter feud with some of his neighbours. This bellicose landowner captured among his prisoners a father and son whom he locked up in a panelled room in the castle. In a frenzy of fear, the father killed his son and then committed suicide by battering his brains out on the wall. Centuries later, when the castle was converted into an hotel, guests constantly complained of seeing the father and son standing by their bedsides and had their blood chilled by dreadful screams which issued from the Oak Room. The old castle is now a Railwaymen's Convalescent Home and it looks as if the good work which is done there has placated the spirits, for there is no recent record of any untoward happenings.

Cheshire has, like Lancashire, its share of animal ghosts and boasts a somewhat less formidable phantom dog than Trash of Formby. Its existence has the unique distinction of being recorded in the minutes of Congleton

Rural Council, for at a meeting of the Council, twenty odd years ago, a letter from a retired farmer was read in which the spectral dog was referred to. The letter, which complained of the condition of a certain field footpath, went on to tell how on rough, dark nights a little white dog bearing a lighted lantern in its mouth used to appear on the path and light people across the field. "It sprang from somewhere and vanished somewhere, but nobody knew where," he wrote, adding that his father had himself seen it scores of times.

Until it was pulled down in 1934, Orchard Cottage at Lower Bebington, was frequently visited by the ghost of a horse. The cottage was at one time occupied by the well-known local antiquary, Mr. E. W. Cox. Time and again, he and his family would hear at midnight the sounds of this horse galloping up to the gate and would rush out to investigate. They never saw any sign of the animal and the closest scrutiny of the ground always failed to reveal any traces of hoofmarks.

The Old Quay House at Parkgate used also to be haunted by a friendly phantom in a red cloak. The house, which at the time of the hauntings was tenanted by Henry Melling, the artist, had, at different periods of its history, done service as a prison and an inn. During the seventeenth and eighteenth centuries, Parkgate was a busy port to which came a continual stream of travellers to and from Ireland, until the shifting of the riversands put an end to the old prosperity. Hundreds of people must have waited for the coach, or for a favourable tide, in the inn, and the ghost may have been that of one of those travellers. On the other hand, it could equally well have been the shade of some former tenant or servant. It might even have been the spirit of one of the earlier prisoners. In any event, during Henry Melling's tenancy, the old lady in the voluminous red cape used to sit silently by the fire in the room occupied by Melling's invalid niece, Clara Payne. Far from being afraid, the bedridden child grew very fond of the gentle ghost, and when the visits suddenly ceased she was missed as keenly as any flesh-and-blood friend.

The nearby village of Neston has a striking story of the mysterious advent of the ghost of a priest who appeared to Teresa Higginson, the famous Merseyside mystic. Miss Higginson, an extremely pious woman, was staying at Neston, and during the absence of the parish priest she took charge of the keys of the Roman Catholic church. Early one morning, a strange priest came to her and intimated without speaking that he wished to say mass in the church. Accordingly, she accompanied him there, unlocked the door and remained in the church with him, hearing mass and receiving Holy Communion from his hands. At the end of the ceremony, Miss Higginson followed the priest into the vestry, only to find it quite empty. The vestments had been neatly folded away but of the celebrant there was not the slightest sign. Thoroughly mystified, Miss Higginson related what had happened to the parish priest upon his return, and he consulted his Bishop. His Lordship recognised the stranger from Miss Higginson's description as a former incumbent whose body had lain buried for many a year in Neston Parish Churchyard.

But the Wirral visitation which affected the largest number of people was undoubtedly that of the Tranmere Terror, which gave the population of Tranmere a week of unrivalled fear. It began one morning when a road watchman reported that his night had been rendered decidedly unpleasant by the sudden appearance of a "gibbering face" which leered into his box from the blackness beyond his brazier. He had, he said, seen no body, and the hideous face seemed to float in the air. By the end of the day, the story had got a solid grip on the public imagination and a first-rate "scare" had developed. When darkness fell, hundreds of people were afraid to venture farther than their own doorsteps and there were almost hourly reports of the apparition's having been seen in one or other of a score of murky alleyways. The scare lasted for about a week, and then stopped abruptly as it had begun. It was never satisfactorily explained, and there are to this day those who will recount with a shudder the tale of that week when the devil came to the suburbs of Birkenhead!

★   ★   ★   ★

What, then does this short survey of Haunted Merseyside amount to! What does it prove?

Footsteps, whisperings, the apparitions which other people claim to have seen and heard—that is not enough.

Time and again, I have gone on a ghost-hunt to this or that allegedly haunted house: always, I have arrived hopeful; always, I have been assured that *this* time it is the real thing; but always, I have left disappointed—a man who would like to believe in ghosts and who is open to be convinced...

7. DEPARTMENT STORE DEATH MASK

Where the lamps quiver
So far in the river,
With many a light
From window and casement,
From garret to basement,
She stood, with amazement,
Houseless by night.

The bleak wind of March
Made her tremble and shiver,
But not the dark arch,
Or the black flowing river:
Mad from life's history,
Glad to death's mystery
Swift to be hurl'd—
Anywhere, anywhere,
Out of the world!

In she plunged boldly,
No matter how coldly,
The rough river ran,—
Over the brink of it,
Picture it—think of it,
Dissolute man!
Lave in it, drink of it,
Then, if you can!

Take her up tenderly,
Lift her with care
Fashion'd so slenderly,
Young and so fair!

The Bridge of Sighs—by THOMAS HOOD.

Innocently pursuing Christmas shopping in a Liverpool department store, I came face to face with a young woman whose body was dragged, dripping, from the Seine perhaps seventy or eighty years ago.

The encounter was scarcely festive: her white face stared up at me from the counter, pallid, pathetic, a little like a head on a mortuary slab.

"The plaques," said the assistant, "they came from Bavaria. We only got three of them. Ever so pretty aren't they? So plain and simple; such good taste; make lovely Christmas gifts."

"Pretty"—but that, in view of what I knew, seemed hardly the right word.

"This is *l'Inconnue de la Seine*," I said, pointing to the little white plaque, "this is a death mask."

The assistant gazed at me uneasily. She cast about an apprehensive eye for the manager. Of course, how should she know? To her it was just another decorative item of Christmas stock. A lovely gift!—this face whose Mona Lisa smile had driven scores of young men and women across the mad frontiers of suicide.

But here is her story, or what little is known of it.

31

L'Inconnue came to us out of the Seine. She gave herself to the river but it rejected her in death even as, one may guess, the city had rejected her in life. They found her, a sorry flotsam, washed up at the water's edge and took her to the Morgue.

We do not know the date of her discovery, but the old Paris Morgue (closed more than twenty years ago) which stood in the square behind Notre Dame at the end of the Ile de la Cité, was rebuilt in 1864, and the style of her hair suggests that she lived sometime in the 'seventies or 'eighties.

In those days the Morgue was one of the sights of Paris. Admission was free, and here gruesome curiosity could be sated with the spectacle of anything between 150 and 200 corpses exhibited on slabs of ice. The purpose of this horrid preservation was to aid in the identification of the bodies of unknowns. Here was gathered the awful harvest of a city's tragedies, seven or eight hundred of them a year; the suicides from the Seine; the hideous relics of the accident; the prey of the murderer; the criminal and his victim, side by side, slab by slab. For three months l'Inconnue lay in this dreadful place: an innocent among a company of horrors. No one came forward. No one claimed her. They discovered nothing about her. Height. Weight. Colour of eyes. Estimated age: 25. That was all. And after that, a pauper's burial, in Père Lachaise it is said.

Once hidden away in the quiet earth, everything would be as if she had never been, vanished like the ripples of the river. But almost at the very end fate took a hand. Unknown in life, unknown in death, this bruised flower of youth was to become a sad species of immortal. The oblivion which she had so hungrily sought was to evade her.

During those last three months, blind chance drove a student from the Ecole des Beaux-Arts, sketch-block in hand, to that store-house of unnatural death. He saw l'Inconnue and was so struck by the haunting loveliness of that delicate, oval face, that he asked permission to cast a death mask. A few weeks later that pathetic creature was laid in her nameless grave, but now innumerable copies of the mask were made. Artists sketched it. Photographs were taken. L'Inconnue was famous.

With neither the virtues of a saint, nor yet the picturesque vices of a sinner in the grand manner, l'Inconnue is something infinitely more subtle— infinitely more dangerous. She is a thing apart. An unhealthy witness to the wisdom of self-destruction. In her closed eyes, in the strange little semi-smile that hovers about her lips—a post-mortem trick of relaxing muscle such as smooths the wrinkles of the elderly dead—impressionable youth has thought to read an invitation to death.

"Come with me," she seems to say, "come with me into the quiet, quiet water-world. Death is not so terrible. See how peacefully I smile in his company. Suicide is the answer," she whispers, "then there is only peace."

She is the Goddess of aimless suicide, the very personification of the mad impulse that flees the lemmings to the sea and appears sinisterly among the young. And about this beckoning image there has grown up a mysterious cult, which reached its peak in the irresponsible 'twenties. In France, Germany and many other countries, young people hurled, slashed and asphyxiated life to a terribly premature conclusion.

What, we wonder, was the tragedy of l'Inconnue.

At this distance of time it has become pointless to enquire. It is difficult to associate her with life; the room she slept in; the clothes she wore; the emotions that coloured her marble face; along with the name she bore, these things are lost. She was poor and unhappy, indisputably. Loved too much, or not enough, she had courage, or cowardice, sufficient to brave icy waters. But perhaps it is better that her riddle remain eternally unsolved. In that way it has potentialities of which fact might cruelly rob it.

For more than half a century now, her head has hung in the studios and attics of the Bohemias of the earth. She is of the world of Trilby and Little Billee, and as long as there are Rudolphs and Marcels, Mimis and Musettes, her memory is in safe-keeping.

And as I carried her plaster shade away from the department store, I could not help wondering in what suburban homes the other two plaques might come to rest. Strange to think of l'Inconnue decorating the pastel-shaded wastes of some bare sitting-room wall. Amusing, that, all-unsuspected, the face of a young French suicide should come to preside over a happy family circle at "Mon Repos."

8. WIGAN'S KIDNAPPED CORPSE

This is a true story of a 74-year-old mystery which started with the death of an earl in Italy, and, after a gruesome little interlude in the wilds of Scotland, reached a satisfactory conclusion in the peace and quiet of Wigan Parish Church. It is the story of an attempt to traffic in a grisly merchandise—an attempt that failed!

Death is usually the end of the chapter; in this case it was only the beginning of a series of incidents so bizarre that they captured the interest and imagination of all Britain.

On December 13th, 1880, the 25th Earl of Crawford, who was also the 8th Earl of Balcarres, died in Florence. In accordance with family tradition, it was decided that his body should be laid to rest in his native land, so the corpse was delivered into the hands of a Florentine chemist who embalmed it in preparation for its long journey back to Scotland.

After embalming, the body was placed in a shell of soft Italian wood: this was encased in lead and the two coffins were then placed in a third of carved oak embellished with chased silver fittings.

Finally, the triple coffin was enclosed in a massive sarcophagus of rich walnut wood upon the top of which was carved a huge cross. Then began the grim Odyssey; a slow and difficult progress across the Alps, a cross-Channel voyage during a gale so heavy that the coffin had to be lashed to the deck, and on by train to Scotland.

It was on Christmas Eve, 1880, that the body reached Aberdeen. There a hearse was waiting to transport it to the late earl's Scottish estate, Dunecht House, where it was to be interred in the newly-erected Mortuary Chapel.

It must have been a weird scene at the station as the men struggled to lift the coffin, which weighed something over half a ton, into the funeral-carriage, especially when it was discovered that the hearse was not large enough to accommodate its monstrous burden, and they had to set to, there and then, to remove the outer sarcophagus.

At last, as dusk began to fall, the task was accomplished; the hearse moved slowly off and was soon lost to sight amid the whirling snow-flakes which all but blinded the driver as he picked a careful way between the stark, frosted hedges lining the tortuous lanes to Dunecht.

The funeral took place five days later, and the earl's remains were reverently laid to rest in the granite fastness of the new mausoleum.

At the conclusion of the service, the mourners, ascending the short flight of eight steps which led up from the vault and watching the four great slabs of granite which sealed the entrance being lowered into place, little dreamed that the melancholy scene they had witnessed was destined to be the prelude to an event which was to cause a thrill of nation-wide horror.

Who, indeed, could possibly have guessed that the peace of that remote crypt was, within a few short months, to be so rudely shattered as to make it the focal point of the attention of the entire English-speaking world.

The first dark hint that all was not well in the vault came on one fine Sunday morning in May 1881. As the housekeeper was returning from the kirk that day, she became aware of a strong aromatic odour which appeared to emanate from the tomb.

The following day, the gardener also noticed this peculiar smell, but, concluding that it came from some wreaths, backed with *arbor vitae*, which lay in withered sympathy upon the dead man's grave, but he did not give the matter very much thought.

In the succeeding days, however, the odour became increasingly pronounced and, as a result of this, the entrance to the crypt was examined and it was found that there was a fissure between two of the outer stones.

Workmen were summoned, the hole was filled in with lime, and there the matter would have ended had it not been for a curious communication which, on September 8th, 1881, was laid upon the desk of Mr. William Yeats, the Crawford family lawyer, at Aberdeen.

This letter bore the Aberdeen postmark and read as follows:—

"Dear Sir,
The remains of the late Earl of Crawford are not beneath the chapel at Dunecht as you believe, but were removed hence last spring, and the smell of decayed flowers ascending from the vault since that time will, on investigation, be found to proceed from another cause than flowers.
NABOB."

After making various enquiries, Mr. Yeats, apparently reassured, dismissed the matter as a practical joke. At the beginning of December 1881, however, the whole affair was brought suddenly and forcibly back into Yeat's mind when some labourers who were working on repairs at Dunecht House summoned him from Aberdeen in respect of an obvious disturbance of the soil covering the vault entrance.

Upon his arrival, Yeats discovered three sets of footprints in the earth and saw a number of spades, picks and other tools scattered about within the railings, which guarded the approach to the mausoleum.

He also observed that one of the slabs had been moved and was now propped up some fifteen or sixteen inches by means of a piece of wood.

Without further ado, Yeats sent for the police. When they arrived they opened the vault, and, descending into it, stumbled upon a scene of nightmare disorder.

The floor was littered with a mixture of sawdust and wood-shavings which gave off the sickly-sweet fragrance which had previously been noted.

The coffins stood in a row, their lids ripped off. They were all empty.

The investigators were glad to escape from that gloomy charnel-house into the fresh air. But they emerged puzzled, for nowhere in all that desecrated tomb could they discover the body of the earl: it had completely vanished.

An intensive search was immediately instituted. Bloodhounds and even clairvoyants were employed, but it was all to no avail. At his wits end, Yeats tried putting an advertisement in the Press:

"Nabob. Please communicate."

Nothing happened. A second appeal was inserted, baited this time with the offer of £50 reward. Ten days later, on December 23rd, 1881, the Earl of Crawford's London solicitors received another letter from "Nabob".

The mysterious correspondent said that he knew the whereabouts of the earl's body but was not disposed to reveal it for fear of being "assinated by rusarectionests."

The weeks turned into months and still the whole affair remained shrouded in mystery, until on July 17th, 1882, an Aberdeen rat-catcher-cum-poacher, named Charles Soutar, was arrested as the result of information laid against him by one George Machray, a game-keeper.

Soutar admitted that he was "Nabob" but persistently denied having had any hand in the abduction of the earl's body.

He told a strange story. He had been poaching near Dunecht House at about 11 o'clock one night at the end of April 1881, he said, when four men had set upon him. Levelling a pistol at his head, one of them had warned him, "Mark this; you're known to our party, and if you breathe a syllable of what you have seen, I will have your life if you are on the face of the earth."

He was then told "Get out," and did so as fast as he could. Overcome with curiosity, he later returned to the spot where he had been assailed.

The men had disappeared, but he noticed a mound of earth where none had been before. Investigating this, he had found to his horror that it contained the body of a man, wrapped in a blanket, and emitting a strange fragrance.

Terrified by what he had seen, he rushed back to Aberdeen, his mind filled with the thought that murder had been done. Remembering the threat of vengeance, he had tried to forget his unpleasant adventure, but a chance meeting with a plasterer named Cowie, at the cattle show in July, had brought it all back to him when the latter happened to mention to him the curious effluvium which was issuing from the Crawford vault. He had then put two and two together and had written the "Nabob" letters.

Having heard this remarkable story, the police went at once to Dunecht and at midnight seventeen of them surrounded the plantation known as Dumbreck Wood which Soutar had described. A thorough search was made with iron probes and by 11-30 the next morning the earl's body had been discovered.

Charles Soutar was subsequently arraigned at the bar of the High Court of Justiciary, Edinburgh. He pleaded not guilty, but after a trial which lasted a day and a half he was found guilty and sentenced to five years penal servitude.

So, the strange case of the kidnapped corpse came to an end. Many people were inclined to think that Soutar was not really guilty, or that, if he were, he had played only a minor part in a drama which was the product of a much higher intelligence.

Whoever conceived and carried out this ghoulish felony, the motive at least is clear—it was for money, and was probably inspired by the recollection of how, in 1878, the corpse of an American millionaire had been snatched from its grave and held to ransom for £25,000.

Ultimately, the body of the 25th Earl of Crawford and Balcarres was reinterred, not in the Dunecht crypt of which he had planned to be the first occupant, but in the family vault beneath the Lindsay Chapel in the beautiful parish church of Wigan, where, to this day, his much-travelled corpse rests happily undisturbed.

9. DEEMING—THE RAINHILL DEMON

The ghastly and murderous saga of Frederick Bailey Deeming, alias Williams, alias Harry Lawson, alias Lord Dunn, self-styled Baron Swanston, self-styled Inspector of Regiments, spans two continents. It begins quietly enough with the birth of a son to a Birkenhead tinsmith in the 1840's, and ends, after a fearful crescendo of murder, in which at least six harmless people lost their lives, on the gallows at Melbourne, Australia, on May 23rd, 1892.

On July 21st, 1891, a stranger alighted from a train at Rainhill and took a room at the Railway Station Hotel. The man, who signed the register as Williams, was about fifty years of age, good-looking in a hard, masculine sort of way, with light-coloured hair, a fair moustache and a stocky, though well-built, body. It was not long before he let it be known among his bar-parlour acquaintances that he was an Inspector of Regiments—a government appointment which appeared to involve a great deal of travelling about and put him on terms of intimacy with all the most important people in the British Empire—and that he was due in a very short time to retire on a princely pension.

Among those who listened with open-mouthed respect to Mr. Williams's tales, none was more impressed than the landlord of the Railway Station Hotel, and it was to him that Williams confided that he was really remaining in the district as a favour to an old friend of his, Baron Brook, who had begged him to find for him a modest but comfortable house within convenient distance of Liverpool.

Now it so happened that a friend of the landlord's, a Mrs. Mather who kept the local newsagent's shop, owned just such a property as Williams seemed to be looking for, and the landlord was proud and happy to effect an introduction. Williams viewed the property—Dinham Villa—and pronounced himself well-satisfied as to its entire suitability. He also viewed Mrs. Mather's pretty 25-year-old daughter, Emily. He was apparently well-satisfied with her, too, for, after the briefest of courtships, he married her.

It was during the salad days of his courtship that a rather unfortunate circumstance threatened to mar that delightful interlude for Mr. Williams. A day or two after he had moved into Dinham Villa, which he was ostensibly preparing for the Baron, a cab drew up outside his handsome front door and disgorged a young woman and four children upon his well-scrubbed step. Their arrival seemed at first to have a distinctly depressing effect upon the ageing Romeo, but he rapidly recovered his usual good spirits and, indeed, made a point of telling all and sundry how nice it was to have his sister and her brood of little ones staying with him, and how lonely it would be when, after a short holiday, she would have to leave to join her husband who was abroad. As a matter of fact, the lady had no intention whatsoever of depriving Williams of the solace of her company for she was his wife.

One afternoon shortly after his "sister's" arrival, Mr. Williams paid a visit to Mrs. Mather and told her that, providing she had no objection, he proposed to make one or two trifling alterations to the villa which he felt would be necessary if the Baron was to be satisfied with his choice. He had noticed, he said, that the floorboards of most of the downstairs rooms were somewhat rough and unevenly laid, and, as the Baron was inordinately proud of a number of exceptionally fine and valuable carpets which he had collected in the course of his travels, he felt that something ought to be done to prevent the possibility of the state of the floors from damaging them. Williams added that he would himself, of course, meet all expenses incurred and explained that it was his intention to take up all the faulty boards and cement the entire surface of the ground beneath them as a precaution against damp. Needless to say, Mrs. Mather thought the idea an excellent one.

So Williams set to work with a will. From a local builder he purchased a pickaxe and several sacks of cement. Unfortunately, his "sister" was not available to help him as, according to the story he told, she had now departed for a sunnier clime. Still, he made the best of things, attending to the cementing himself and engaging a carpenter to help with the re-laying of the boards.

Once that floor was finally set in order, Williams seemed much relieved. He celebrated the completion of the work with a discreet little party. Light refreshments were served; healths were drunk; there was dancing across the smooth new boards, and, as the evening drew to its happy close, Williams set the seal to a merry occasion by asking Emily Mather if she would consent to become his wife. With many a pretty blush, she accepted his proposal.

No sooner was their marriage arranged, than the Baron became unaccountably awkward and decided that his pressing need for a house in the vicinity of Liverpool had ceased to exist. An apologetic Mr. Williams accordingly vacated Dinham Villa and took up his abode in Mrs. Mather's house pending the celebration of his nuptials.

A few weeks after their wedding, Williams told his bride that his duties as an Inspector of Regiments necessitated their immediate departure for Australia. There, the Williams's moved into a small furnished house at Windsor, a suburb of Melbourne, and barely had they unpacked their bags when Mr. Williams became suddenly and unaccountably dissatisfied with the state of the dining-room floor. Up came the boards, down went some cement and, by the most amazing coincidence, Mr. Williams's second wife vanished from the scene.

Practice makes perfect they say, but Williams's second attempt at floor-laying was by no means an improvement on his first. So bad a job did he make of it in fact that when, soon after his wife's disappearance, Williams left the house, the owner felt obliged to take a hand at this re-laying business himself. The results of this little essay in floor-fixing were to prove disastrous for Mr. Williams, for beneath the cement was discovered the corpse of his wife.

At the time of Mrs. Williams's resurrection her sorrowing husband was on the verge of marrying again, but the police soon put a stop to that. While he was cooling his ardour in an Australian gaol, the Melbourne police communicated with the Lancashire Constabulary who promptly made their way to Dinham Villa where they, too, embarked upon what seems to have been the ubiquitously popular pastime of pulling up the floor.

What their excavations revealed may be said to have tied the knot in the rope which was already round Williams's neck. A foot below the cement were huddled the bodies of a woman and four children. The news spread rapidly, creating a sensation paralleled only in modern times by the laying bare in Notting Hill's Rillington Place of the gruesome secrets of Christie's kitchen. It was a macabre touch that, in the ensuing rush for newspapers, as the only newsagent in the Rainhill district at that time, it was Mrs. Mather who was obliged to sell the reports of her daughter's death in Australia and of the further terrible evidence against the man she married that was being uncovered at Dinham Villa.

Meanwhile, the Sydney police recollected a similar discovery which had been made beneath the floor of a house in their city some two or three years previously, following the disappearance of another Mrs. Williams and her two children. That mystery had never been satisfactorily cleared up, and it was decided that the Mr. Williams now languishing in Melbourne Gaol was undoubtedly the author of that characteristic little piece of skulduggery too.

Frederick Deeming's trial opened on May 8th, 1892, at Melbourne Criminal Court.

Standing there in the dock, Deeming was at last occupying the position to which all his life of murder and make-believe had inexorably been leading.

The youngest of seven children, he had early disappointed his worthy, if humble, parents, by his persistent refusal to remain in any of a series of jobs which had been found for him. For a while his father had supported him in idleness, until at length he had become a steward on one of the tall ships and set forth to see the world.

For several years his family heard nothing of him, and then he suddenly reappeared bedecked with costly-looking jewellery, flashing a well-filled wallet and full of tales of the rich harvest of the South African goldfields.

He remained home just long enough to savour the envy and admiration of friends and family and then was away again.

Australia, New Zealand, South Africa and America were all ports of call in his criminous Odyssey where he managed to pick up in various shady ways the money which he required for his personal adornment, the support of a succession of brassy women friends and the satisfaction of his craving to make an impression. After many years of these fitful comings and goings, Deeming at last brought home a wife and child to meet his parents and informed them that he and his family were off to settle in Australia.

It was not long, however, before he had deserted his young wife and was off on his travels once more.

News of Deeming comes next from Europe. He stayed briefly in Antwerp, where he was known to the smart set as Lord Dunn. But some chicanery or other necessitated His Lordship's hurried departure, and it was as Harry Lawson, wealthy Australian sheep-farmer, that the protean Deeming next appeared at Beverley, near Hull.

Here, he lived in a good-class boarding-house, contrived to "marry" the proprietress's daughter, perpetrated a spectacular series of swindles on Hull jewellers, booked a passage to Montevideo and was on the high seas before his frauds were discovered.

This time he was not to escape. He was arrested when he landed at Montevideo, brought back to England and sent to prison for nine months.

Free once again, he made his way to Rainhill where, as we have seen, the wife and family he had abandoned caught up with him and were promptly murdered for their pains.

Strangely enough, Deeming was never tried for the Rainhill killings, but he was found guilty of the murder of Emily Mather at Windsor and sentenced to death.

He divided his time in gaol between considerations of his fate in this world and the next, alternately indulging in the purely practical exercise of making neat little drawings of gibbets and the reading of the Bible.

Outwardly calm and cheerful, some clue to the state of his inner feelings is afforded by the fact that during those last weeks his hair turned snow-white.

It was a lovely morning when, on May 23rd, 1892, Deeming strolled out to the scaffold, smoking a large cigar, which had been given him by the executioner, and chatting amiably with the prison officials.

Surely fate played a strange trick on him at the end when it selected Swanston Gaol as the place where the man who had so often called himself Baron Swanston was deftly despatched upon the last of his many journeys.

10. THE CURIOUS CASE OF DOCTOR CLEMENTS

When Amy Victoria Clements, the 47-year-old fourth wife of Dr. Robert George Clements, the well-known physician, surgeon and gynaecologist, died at Southport, in May 1947, few of those who sympathised with the doctor in his sad bereavement could have foreseen the triple tragedy of which her death was but the first.

To all intents and purposes there was, superficially, nothing suspicious about her end: Mrs. Clements had lost her life as the result of natural causes. The unfortunate lady had died of a rare blood disease known as *myeloid leukaemia*. That, at any rate, was the verdict of Dr. J. M. Houston, the brilliant young pathologist who performed the post-mortem.

The funeral was arranged to take place at Christ Church, Southport, on the morning of Friday, May 30th, 1947, and it came as a severe shock to the assembled mourners when the vicar, the Reverend F. H. Pilkington, announced that the service would have to be postponed as it had been decided that an inquest was to be held.

As a matter of fact, two further shocks were in store for them, for it transpired that at the very time that they had been waiting at the church the doctor himself had been dying of a self-administered overdose of morphine and, two days later, the young pathologist, Dr. Houston, took his own life.

Naturally, these curious circumstances provoked an intense public interest, and the dead doctor and his affairs were subjected to the searchlight of a close scrutiny. The facts which emerged from this investigation did not redound altogether to the doctor's credit and, indeed, indicated that the gentleman had been something of a marital adventurer.

It was shortly after graduating from Queen's University, Belfast, in 1904, that Robert Clements made his first essay in matrimony. The woman he married was ten years his senior and the daughter of a wealthy Belfast miller. She died in 1920, and her widower himself signed her death certificate—an unorthodox, though not illegal, procedure. She died intestate, leaving less than £11, although she was said to have inherited about £25,000 from her father only a few years previously.

After this, the wagging of tongues made Belfast a not altogether pleasant place for Dr. Clements' continued residence, and presently he moved to Moss Side, Manchester, where, after discarding the top-hat and white spats which he had always worn in Ireland, he settled down with a colleen from County Antrim as his second wife. She lasted for just five years, and then succumbed to what her husband certified as endocarditis, leaving £425 which soon found its way into the doctor's bank account.

For the next three years Dr. Clements led a carefree bachelor existence until, in 1928, Kathleen Sarah Burke fell beneath the sway of the undoubted Clements' charm and agreed to share her life with him. The third Mrs. Clements survived, apparently happy and healthy for precisely eleven years, and then, in 1939, she died, somewhat suddenly, at Southport of what her grieving husband certified as cancer. The doctor benefited from her death to the extent of £489. In consequence of a communication which they received, the police decided to make a closer examination of the corpse of the deceased woman, but they were too late. Even as they telephoned to the Liverpool Crematorium, Kathleen Clement's body was being consumed by the flames.

One would have thought that after that the doctor's next wife might have stood a slightly better chance of attaining to old age, but not a bit of it. A few months after Kathleen's demise, Dr. Clements was once again mouthing vows to love, honour and cherish at the altar-rails. This time he took to himself Amy Victoria Barnett, the daughter of a rich Lancashire company director, to whom he had been paying considerable, and by no means unremarked, attention even during the lifetime of his previous wife. The fourth wedding was a very grand affair and took place in London at St. George's, Hanover Square.

Back in Southport after the honeymoon, the couple settled down to what seems to have been an agreeable, if somewhat humdrum, life. The doctor is remembered by those who knew him during the eight years preceding his wife's death as a courtly, charming man, something of a dandy in his dress and a great church-goer. There must, however, have been at least one person who descried beneath this affable exterior the cold, calculating nature of the smiling doctor, for scarcely was Mrs. Clements' body cold when the police received, for the second time, a communication.

It was addressed to Mr. C. Bolton, the West Lancashire Coroner. Mr. Bolton acted at once, and having ordered the cancellation of the funeral, he promptly called in two Home Office experts, Dr. J. B. Firth and the late Dr. W. H. Grace. These two gentleman soon found themselves somewhat hamstrung in their investigations because the organs which had been removed from the dead woman's body at the post-mortem had been subsequently burned. But Dr. Firth, who undertook the chemical analyses, is not the sort of man to let a little thing like that stand in his way. One kidney remained, and after a great deal of painstaking work Firth succeeded in discovering about one-third of a grain of morphine in it. Thus encouraged, he set to work sawing sections of her vertebrae which he carried off to his laboratory at Preston. After the best part of a week's activity, and a good deal of abstruse mathematical calculation, Dr. Firth announced that about one-twentieth of a grain of morphine was also present in the woman's spine. The matter was clinched by his discovery of morphine crystals in Dr.

Clement's hypodermic syringe and the fact that some tablets in a bottle of what should have been a phenobarbitone preparation turned out to be morphine.

In the circumstances, it is hardly to be wondered at that the jury did not need very much time in order to find that Dr. Clements had murdered his wife and then committed *felo-de-se*. As the murderer was already dead there was no question of proceeding any further, but, the mere mechanics of the murder resolved, there remained, and still remains, the psychological problem as to motive.

Was the doctor, victim of an overpowering greed, simply after his wife's money? Or was it, perhaps, that things had come to such a pitch between them that he could no longer endure to live with her? We shall never know. But it may be that the rather pathetic remark which he made on one occasion, "I can't remember when I ate a cooked meal in my own flat," contains more than a germ of the truth.

11. POLTERGEIST OVER RUNCORN

It is just three years since, on a wet Sunday night, I kept a date with a poltergeist.

A dressing-table danced in the dark; a clock flew through the air; a boy was hit by a drawer and flung roughly out of bed. A poltergeist had come to Runcorn.

Suddenly and alarmingly, on Sunday, August 10th, 1952, *something* entered a quiet household at Number 1 Byron Street and shattered the peaceful lives of the inhabitants of that undistinguished little house in a Runcorn back street. That night 68-year-old Mr. Sam Jones and his 17-year-old grandson, John Glynn, retired as usual to the bedroom which they shared. Scarcely had the light been put out, when they were disturbed by a scratching sound in a drawer of the dressing-table. Thinking at first that it must be a mouse, they got up to investigate, but could find nothing to account for the noise. No sooner were they back in bed, however, than the scratching began again. On succeeding nights there were other and far more violent occurrences. A ponderous dressing-table began to rock giddily. Loud knockings hammered the stillness. A clock shattered itself against the wall. Invisible hands hurled books across the room. A stout blanket-chest, weighing at least half a hundredweight, reared itself into the air and a water-jug and basin shivered into fragments.

Naturally, such happenings could not be hushed up. Gradually the news spread. Who or what was the agent of this mysterious havoc? That was the question on everyone's lips and it was not long before the word "Poltergeist" was being whispered uneasily from street to street. Soon, all Runcorn was divided into hotly arguing factions of sceptics and believers. Everywhere, the Byron Street hauntings became number one talking-point. At quiet firesides, in countless little kitchens and in loud-humming bars, puzzled locals discussed the amazing manifestations which were focusing nation-wide attention on that insignificant street. Never before had the little Cheshire township (pop 24,000) witnessed such events, and its bleak, chemical-soaked atmosphere became positively electric as this quiet place of tanneries, chemical factories and shipbuilding yards saw itself hurled into the headlines.

And all the while the strange things went on happening in Byron Street. Police, clergymen and interested neighbours were invited to investigate. They came; they saw and unanimously they pronounced: "The occurrences are very weird and unusual. We do not think it is a hoax." Local police set traps to catch a joker. They failed. Spiritualist Phil France held a three-hour seance in the room. "It is definitely a poltergeist," he announced when he emerged. Then, Widnes Methodist minister, the Reverend W. H. Stevens, a member of the Society for Psychical Research, came on the scene. Armed with a notebook and various articles of scientific impedimenta, he kept vigil in the house. After experiencing a number of unaccountable phenomena and being hit on the head by a flying dictionary, he said: "Things are beyond a joke. There is no question of this being a hoax."

Such was the state of affairs when, seven weeks after their commencement, I drove over to Runcorn to assess the situation for myself. By that time the family had grown rather tired of all the publicity, but eventually they agreed to let me spend the night in the haunted room. The scene of the alleged manifestations was a small, bare bedroom on the first floor and the trouble was said to begin as soon as John Glynn and his friend John Berry, who was staying with him for company, retired to bed. That night everything went according to schedule. Shortly after 11 o'clock I went upstairs and carefully examined the room. I found no evidence of trickery— no wires or anything of that kind. The boys clambered into the big double bed which they shared and the solitary, naked bulb lighting the room was snapped out. About two minute later there came a terrific crash from the dressing-table. "There it is," said John Glynn. The words were barely out of his mouth when a small alarm-clock was thrown violently across the room. I remained for several hours witnessing all manner of superficially abnormal events. The poltergeist, I was told, performed only in total darkness and it became very temperamental when I started to wander about with my torch at the ready. Furthermore, I found that of all the alleged phenomena which took place that night NOT ONE was of such a nature that it could not have been perpetrated by human agency from the bed—dressing-table, clock, drawer, books and so forth, were all within easy reach of the boys. Indeed, on one occasion a sudden stabbing ray from my torch revealed the protruded arm of John Glynn being swiftly withdrawn from the direction whence a "spirit knock" had just sounded. After that, the poltergeist appeared to be somewhat uncertain of itself, and once it was perceived that I was hovering in very close proximity both to the boys and the furniture, manifestations were few and cautious. Most significant, perhaps, was the complete lack of any atmosphere of fear which I am assured is the inevitable accompaniment of all well-attested instances of psychic phenomena.

Ghost or hoax? That was, and still is, the question. At the time, I felt pretty sure that I could have found the answer if I had been permitted to bind the hands and feet of the two boys and remove all possible accomplices from the room. Unfortunately, I was not able to do any of those things and in the circumstances felt that conditions were far from foolproof.

In fairness, however, I must say that measured against the yardstick of accumulated data from hundreds of previously observed instances of poltergeist infestation, the Runcorn case presented many typical features.

The pattern of events in all these visitations is astonishingly constant. Suddenly, for no ascertainable reason, some ordinary little house becomes the focus of a terrifying drama. One night the family is disturbed by a minor and completely inexplicable irritation—a gentle but insistent tapping, scratching or something of the sort. Natural causes are searched for, but cannot be found; natural explanations are hopefully sought, but are not forthcoming. Invariably, an adolescent is present in the house and it is soon obvious that he or she is the centre of the disturbances. They occur only when this person is at home and most frequently when he gets into bed. On subsequent nights there are further and more unnerving incidents. Objects are thrown about, furniture rocks, the boy's face is slapped by invisible hands, all to the hideous accompaniment of sundry bumps and crashings. At first, everyone is filled with fear, but, as they grow more accustomed to these uncanny happenings, the fear gives way to anger, and, at length, anger to a kind of strained familiarity. The intruder is given a nickname—in the Runcorn case it was christened "Jooker"—and becomes the subject of half-hearted joking. The vicar is called in and for long hours holds bewildered vigil amidst the old-fashioned furniture of the crowded living-room. Neighbours begin to talk. The local paper paramounts the story. There are inquisitive callers, and, by a strange psychological quirk, the victims become almost proud of their tormentor, jealous to preserve it from the stigma of fraud. But this phase rapidly passes and is followed by an attitude of mute despair which persists until, as suddenly as it came, the poltergeist departs for ever.

As I left the little house in Byron Street in the small hours of the morning, I found myself wondering how long that persecuted family would have to wait for their deliverance. Outside, it was still raining and small groups of sightseers were scattered in shivering tufts upon the shining pavement; just standing quietly in the dark, looking up at John Glynn's window while a couple of weary-eyed policemen vainly urged them to move along bedwards.

Now, three years later, I have been back to Runcorn and I have learned the end of the story. By October 1952, the disturbances had become so frequent and violent that the family were obliged to sleep out at various friends' houses. On October 17th an element of tragedy was introduced, for Miss Nellie Whittle, an elderly spinster who lodged in that unquiet house, plunged to her death on Runcorn Hill. I do not suggest that this was necessarily connected with the hauntings for, although poltergeist seem to have a morbid liking for homes where people are very ill or dying, it is not often that their presence is related to murder, suicide or death of any sort.

Then there was the business of the pigs. Mr. Sam Jones was working for Mr. Crowther of Pool Farm, Runcorn. One day in the middle of August,

47

for no apparent reason, three of Mr. Crowther's pedigree pigs died. At the end of a fortnight every one of his fifty-three pigs were dead. Five veterinary surgeons examined the bodies and were totally unable to account for these mysterious deaths. Two days after the loss of the last pig, Mr. Crowther was astonished to see what he descibed to me as "a large black cloud about seven feet in height, shapeless except for two prongs sticking out at the back," coming straight down his yard. He mentioned this curious experience to no one, but, three days later, his wife told him that she had seen something which corresponded precisely with his own vision, floating about the yard. One evening some weeks afterwards, Mr. Crowther actually discovered the cloud-like apparition in his kitchen. He brushed past it as he made for the light switch, and, as he did so, the two prongs, which felt "solid, like blunt sticks," went for his throat. As soon as he switched on the light the cloud disappeared. It was about this time that Mr. Crowther, at Sam Jones's urgent request, went to the house in Byron Street, and there, hovering above John Glynn's bed, he saw to his horror, the same forked cloud. It was on December 13th, 1952, that Mr. Crowther encountered the cloud for the last time. He had just let his two dogs out of a shed. They rushed forth barking frenziedly, and, turning, he saw beside him the cloud, which appeared lighter in colour and considerably smaller than previously. It moved rapidly along the ground, the dogs barking and jumping at it, and then rose high into the air and disintegrated.

By a strange coincidence, it was in fact round about this time that the Byron Street hauntings suddenly ceased. Appropriately enough, the poltergeist's very last effort was to fold up the carpet! John Glynn went into the army in the following January but he had a nervous breakdown, which was attributed to the strain of the experiences which he had undergone during the four months of poltergeistic persecution, and army psychiatrists recommended his discharge.

And so the pattern was complete. Conforming to precedent, the poltergeist has departed. Today, peace is restored to the little house in Byron Street. The whole unhappy business has passed into local legend, something to be talked about in hushed voices round winter hearths; something which remains only as a record in the yellowing pages of the files of one of those little local papers which are the rich archives of thousands of similar poltergeistic paradoxes.

12. WONDERS FROM A DEAD MAN'S HAND

From hundreds of miles the lame, the halt and the blind come, with faith in their hearts, for the healing touch of a dead man's hand.

As we sat in the comfortable parlour of his 55-year-old presbytery at Ashton-in-Makerfield, Canon R. W. Meagher told me the fascinating and seemingly miraculous story of the Holy Hand.

On the table before him were five letters—that morning's post. They came from Liverpool, Leeds, Sheffield, Burnley and Whittle-le-Woods, and the writers all had the same request to make. Would the Canon send them a small piece of linen which had been in contact with the wonder-working relic. And every day the Canon's postbag bulges with letters of this sort, some of which come from as far afield as Valparaiso. But they are not always requests for help. Sometimes, there is a letter which tells a story of triumph.

"Here," said Canon Meagher, "is one which I received only yesterday." Upon a small sheet of paper was written the joyous testimony of a woman from Slough in Buckinghamshire. Last November she had brought her ailing 7-year-old son to the Church of St. Oswald, King and Martyr, at Ashton-in-Makerfield, to be blessed by the Holy Hand. Now, she was writing to say that the child was making "'remarkable strides towards recovery" and she added that "the doctor said it was a miracle." And this is no isolated incident; for close on 300 years such cures have been reported.

To whom does this hand belong and how came it to the beautiful church on the hill in the little Lancashire mining town where pit shorts and clogs are to be seen in the shop-windows?

It is now 327 years since that shrivelled hand was supple with life, and its owner, Blessed Edmund Arrowsmith, Roman Catholic priest, and martyr, paid the supreme price for his faith in the old priest-hunting days of the Reformation.

The young Arrowsmith was born, in 1585, at Garswood near Haydock, which was in the parish of Winwick, about half-way between Wigan and Warrington. His father Robert Arrowsmith, was a yeoman farmer, whose wife, Margery, was of the ancient house of Gerard. Both of Arrowsmith's parents were staunch recusants and the sturdy Lancashire countryside of the days of Elizabeth Tudor, though then a place of lovely farms and mellow homesteads, a countryside as yet unscarred by coal-pits and the tall, black stacks of factory chimneys, was no bed of roses for those of papistic persuasions.

Indeed, while Edmund Arrowsmith (who, by the way, was christened Bryan and did not take the name Edmund until later in life) was still a small child he had an early taste of what his faith would cost him. One night the pursuivants forced their way into the Arrowsmith home, dragged the child out of his cot and left him shivering in his nightshirt as they carried his parents off to Lancaster Gaol as practising Papists. Fortunately, some kind neighbours took the child into their home and looked after him until his parents were released.

Wearied at last with repeated imprisonments and the huge fines which were the only alternative, Robert Arrowsmith fled with his family to Belgium. There he was almost immediately conscripted into the Protestant ranks, probably in the English army which Queen Elizabeth had sent under her favourite Leicester to aid the Netherlands in their revolt against the Spanish rule which had rapidly developed into a religious war between Protestants and Catholics. When Sir William Stanley with his Irish regiment passed over to the Spanish side, Arrowsmith followed suit.

After that, Robert made his way to the English College of Douai where his brother, Edmund, was a distinguished professor of theology. He then decided to return to his native Lancashire where, shortly afterwards, he died.

Her husband's death left Margery Arrowsmith in somewhat straitened circumstances and a kindly priest offered to take Edmund off her hands. The arrangement was that in return for the lad's services about the house the priest would teach him grammar.

When the boy was twenty, he crossed the Channel and entered the College of Douai. After a stay of two years he became seriously ill and had to return to Lancashire. Restored in health, he was subsequently sent back to Douai by the good priest who had previously been his master and was able to complete his interrupted classical studies. It was during a spiritual retreat at the end of his course of philosophy that Edmund decided to become a priest. He received minor orders in St. Nicholas's Church, Douai, on June 14th, 1612, and on the following December 9th was consecrated priest in Arras.

Father Arrowsmith was now twenty-seven years old, and he returned to England as a member of the English Mission. For the next ten years he worked hard among English Roman Catholics. Then, suddenly, he was arrested and thrown into Lancaster Goal. He was fortunate that he came up for trial at a time when the persecution was somewhat relaxed. A Royal match was then being proposed between Prince Charles and a Spanish princess and Father Arrowsmith received the mercy of release.

He spent the succeeding nine years working with zeal and virtue as a secular priest, and finally achieved a long-standing ambition to become a Jesuit in 1624.

It was on a summer's morning in 1628 that the fate which had been foreshadowed by his childhood experience finally overtook Edmund Arrowsmith. It came about in this way. A certain Mr. Holden in Lancashire had married his first cousin, who was a Protestant, before a minister. He later applied to Father Arrowsmith for a dispensation, which, after much discussion, he agreed to give upon the condition that the couple separated for a fortnight before the Catholic marriage service was celebrated. This infuriated the Holdens, and in the height of their anger they denounced the Jesuit to a magistrate named Rostern and told him that the priest could be found at the Blue Anchor Inn in Hoghton Straits which was owned by Holden's father. By the time the pursuivants reached the Blue Anchor Father Arrowsmith had flown, but his horse got into a bog and he was taken prisoner. His captors bore him to a Hoghton alehouse (now the Boar's Head) where he was stripped to the skin, subjected to every infamy and had his pockets emptied for nine shillings which sum was entirely dissipated on drink in an hour!

Then it was back to Lancaster Gaol. The Oath of Supremacy was tendered to him. He refused it. The magistrates committed him to take his trial at the next asize.

On August 26th, 1628, Judge Sir Henry Yelverton summoned Father Arrowsmith to the bar.

"Sirrah," said the Judge, "are you a priest?"

"I would I were," replied Arrowsmith. To own his sacerdotal character would have been to bring disaster on his hosts.

"Yes," said Sir Henry, "though he is not, yet he desires to be a traitor; this fact makes him guilty."

The judge asserted that the prisoner could say nothing in behalf of his faith. That was too much for Father Arrowsmith. "I will not only defend it by words, but would gladly seal it with my blood," he flashed back.

"You *shall* seal it with your blood," barked Sir Henry. "You shall die," he said again and again.

"And you too, my Lord, must die," retorted Arrowsmith.

Found guilty of high treason, Arrowsmith was sentenced by Sir Henry as follows: "You shall go from hence to the place from whence you came, from thence you shall be drawn on a hurdle to the place of execution. You shall then be hanged by the neck till you be half dead; your bowels shall be burnt and your quarters shall be set on the four corners of the Castle. And may God have mercy on you."

Father Arrowsmith hearing this sank on his knees and said, "Thanks be to God." Whereupon the ferocious judge sent the sheriff to bid the gaoler to load the prisoner with the heaviest fetters he could find and to lock him up alone in the darkest dungeon.

On August 28th, 1628, 43-year-old Edmund Arrowsmith died valiantly at Lancaster. After being dragged through the streets upon a hurdle, he mounted the ladder to the gibbet, the ladder turned, his body fell, but he was dead before the awful drawing and quartering began. His severed head was placed on the tower of Lancaster Castle and his quarters were taken from the cauldron in which they had been boiled and hung up at the Castle.

Doubtless, it was one of Arrowsmith's relatives who salvaged his right hand from the grim remains at the Castle one dark night and brought it to his sorrowing mother.

Then strange things began to happen. Sick people claimed that they had been restored to health by the magic touch of the martyr's hand. In 1736 a crippled boy was able to throw away his crutches after the Holy Hand had been applied to his stricken limbs.

In 1832 a young girl named Mary Selby had a withered arm restored to use by the touch of Blessed Edmund Arrowsmith's hand. A poor woman awaiting an operation for cancer of the breast in Bournemouth Infirmary in 1893, had taken to her a piece of linen which had touched the Holy Hand. She applied it to her breast and when that very morning the surgeon came to perform the operation he found that the tumour had completely vanished. Again, the story is told of how, many years ago, the owner of nearby Ince Hall was very anxious to make a new will, but he died before his lawyer arrived. The lawyer, however, sent for the Holy Hand with which he rubbed the dead hand of his client which immediately seized a pen and signed the document.

Sometime during the 1850's, the Gerard family delivered the hand of their ancestor into the safe-keeping of a pious villager who became known as the Custodian of the Holy Hand, and in the 1870's it was given into the custody of the church.

And all down the years cure after cure has taken place. Catholics, non-Catholics, sceptics and believers, all have benefited equally, AND CURES ARE STILL TAKING PLACE. Canon Meagher told me that every week sees scores of hopeful pilgrims wending their way to his church, and each Sunday afternoon at 3-30 he blesses those who congregate in St. Oswald's with the Holy Hand.

We made our way into the church and the Canon led me to where, in a small apse at the rear of the main altar, the precious relic is kept. The priest unlocked the wrought-iron gates which guard Blessed Edmund's shrine and I saw a silver-gilt tabernacle gleaming in the reredos of a small altar. Taking a key from beneath his black and scarlet cassock, the Canon unlocked the reliquary and drew forth the Holy Hand. It was enclosed in a hermetically sealed crystal case. At one time it was simply wrapped in linen and kept in a silken bag, but it had started to wear out from constant touching. As I held the 300-year-old hand in my own, I noticed how small and extraordinarily delicate it was. Brown and withered, the strips of parboiled flesh adhering to it looked like old leather, but the finger-nails were perfectly preserved. I asked Canon Meagher point-blank if he thought that this tragic relic really was imbued with some strange supernatural power. He hesitated a moment or two and then said, "All I can say is that I have been greatly impressed by the evidence that I have seen, but my church will not ascribe the term 'miraculous' to any object until its powers have been fully investigated and proved beyond any reasonable shadow of doubt." Nevertheless, the Roman Church beatified Edmund Arrowsmith on December 15th, 1929. Whether or not he will at some future date be canonised, is a question which only time will answer. But meanwhile hundreds of people whom the doctors cannot help, continue to find new hope in the workings of a relic whose powers are undoubtedly strange beyond the understanding of this world.

13. THE MYSTERY HOUSE OF MULGRAVE STREET

One of the things that always strikes me as rather a pity is that history as we know it invariably confines itself to the chronicling of great events. It is wonderfully precise regarding the dates and doings of kings and queens and windy statesmen, but turns a glory-blinded eye to the thousands of little everyday details that go to make up the background of an age. Unless it be in the published memoirs or diaries of contemporaries, or the ephemeral effusion of the journalist, these fascinating trivia have no memorial. They are forever lost or, worse, pass down by word of mouth, distorted beyond all recognition, and thus useless as history. A case in point is that of the Mystery House of Mulgrave Street whose strange story has, down the years, become part of the hitherto unwritten folklore of Liverpool.

★   ★   ★   ★

Like many another of my generation, I heard the story of the tragic bride of Mulgrave Street at my mother's knee. I listened to it spell-bound, and along with all the other nursery tales of giants and witches, of fairies good and bad, I accepted it unquestioningly. When I grew older the world soon robbed me of my childish belief in ogres, augurs and fairy-godmothers, but the legend of Mulgrave Street lingered on in the misty hinterland of my mind. It was not, in fact, until quite recently that it even occurred to me that it might possibly belong to the realm of fable.

I don't suppose I had given the old story a thought for twenty years until, lunching at my club the other day, a friend suddenly said to me, "I'm surprised you've never written-up the history of the Mystery House of Mulgrave Street." For a moment I was puzzled, and then all at once it came back to me.

At a time when I still relied upon a perambulator rather than my own two legs to convey me, peripatetic, around the streets of Liverpool, we lived in an old and rather splendid house in Upper Parliament Street. I was a somewhat delicate child and the doctor had told my parents that I should get as much fresh air as possible. On sunny afternoons I was, therefore, usually wheeled along the Boulevard to Prince's Park, but on dull days when lowering skies drooped grey with the threat of rain, my nurse would venture no farther afield with me than a hurried promenade as far as Crown Street and back. It was on those occasions, I remember, that we used to pass a dreary, three-story, red brick house whose dust-curtained windows lent to it a forlorn and distinctly sinister aspect. The house stood on the corner of Mulgrave and Upper Parliament streets, and my nurse, a superstitious Irish girl, would always scurry past it with piously averted eyes. So far as I could discover, no one had ever been within its forbidding walls, but I gathered that it was the home of an old, old lady who had once been engaged to be married. On her wedding-morning the bride had waited at the church for the groom in vain. He never turned up, and the heartbroken girl returned alone to the house where the wedding-breakfast lay waiting. She went in, closed the door behind her and never again emerged. From that day onwards the house remained shuttered and lifeless, the table still laid, the feast turning to dust, the sorrowing bride gradually changing from a lovely young girl into an old wrinkled woman in a yellowing wedding-dress. All this I learned from my nurse, and my mother afterwards confirmed that the extraordinary tale had been current when she was a child, and added that to her certain knowledge that eerie old house had stood with its blank unlit windows and smokeless chimneys, lonely and deserted for as long as she could remember.

★ ★ ★ ★

After that lunch-time conversation with my friend, in the course of which I discovered that he had heard, and always believed, exactly the same story as I had, I made a point of asking everyone I met if they knew anything about the house in question. Most of them did. And it was always the same thing. A jilted bride had forsaken the world to live alone in a house of memories where the wedding-breakfast crumbled to dust. The thing became an obsession and I decided that I must find out once and for all whether or not there was any truth in it.

I began by going alone to the house. I found it far from lifeless. It has now been converted into flats and the voices of children have put the ghosts of the past to flight. I had a bit of difficulty in deciding whether it is really in Mulgrave Street or Upper Parliament Street, for it stretches right round the corner, and one of the tenants told me that it is regarded as both number 1 Mulgrave Street *and* number 166 Upper Parliament Street.

My next step was to make a careful search through the mouldering pages of a formidable pile of ancient Gore's Liverpool Directories. Number 166 Upper Parliament Street makes its first appearance in the street directory for the year 1880. It was then apparently a newly-erected house, and its first occupant was a Mr. Richard Holden Davis, described as an alkali manufacturer (Golding, Davis & Co.), who, prior to moving in there, had lived at number 16 Montpellier Terrace, which is just across the road. He seems to have lived at number 166 alone until 1898, when he was joined there by one Richard H. Davidson, an oil refiner of the firm of Richard Davidson & Co., of 24 Maguire Street. The following year two more gentlemen arrived, a Mr. Herbert S. Davidson and another Richard Davidson, both described as oil refiners. In 1900 all four are still in residence, but the original Richard Holden Davis is now described as 'gentleman', by

55

which we are presumably to understand that he has now retired from alkali manufacturing. By 1901, Joseph M. Davidson, clerk, has taken up quarters at number 166, but Richard H. Davidson has moved out to Aigburth. Throughout 1902 the *ménage à quatre* remains unchanged, but in 1903 a Miss M. R. Davis is listed as occupier of the property, and Messrs. Richard, Herbert S., and Joseph M. Davidson have all moved to Manor House, Promenade, Liscard. Miss M. R. Davis's name continues to appear in 1904, 1905 and, for the last time, in 1906, as sole tenant.

It was in March, 1906, I discovered, that, after a long illness, Richard Holden Davis died. He is buried in Smithdown Road Cemetery. From another source I learned that just before his death Mr. Davis gave the house to his maiden sister, Miss M. R. Davis, who was then about 40 years of age, and who had, no doubt, acted as his nurse.

After the death of her brother, to whom she was deeply attached, Miss Davis felt that she could not continue to live in the house which was large and full of painful memories for her. But neither could she bring herself to sell it or disturb its contents. She therefore kept it fully furnished, but closed it up and took rooms nearby. From time to time she would go in there, always alone. All the charges on the house were duly paid, and it was kept in a good state of repair. When, for instance, a chimney-stack blew down in a storm, it was rebuilt in a matter of two days. For 26 years things continued thus, and a mystified local populace, inspired maybe by memories of Dickens's Miss Havisham, invented the story of the tragic bride.

Somewhere about 1931 Miss Davis must have died—it is said that she ended her days with a nephew in Birkenhead—and in 1932 the old house reappears in Kelly's Directory. It had been bought by the Prudential Assurance Company, and from then until 1935 was occupied by three successive superintendents in the employ of that company.

Although number 166 Upper Parliament Street never again appears in the Liverpool directory after 1934, there is no reason to suppose that it underwent any further period of emptiness, and no one seeing its bright and cheerful countenance to-day would ever suspect that strange episode in its history when for more than a quarter of a century it stood silent and withdrawn, a lonely place of ghosts and a legendary abode of mystery.

14. A STRANGE EPISODE IN THE HISTORY OF A CHURCH

TWENTY or so feet up on the red brick face of an unobtrusive church on the darker side of Upper Parliament Street, there is a largish arched recess. Empty now, it looks as if it should contain a statue, and once upon a time it did—that of a woman with a babe in her arms.

In a way, the disappearance of that statue was closely linked with certain dark events which took place thirty-four years before—a strange episode in the history of a church which led to the violent deaths of two men and a woman.

★　★　★　★

The story begins on the first day of the year 1883, when there was opened in Falkland Street, off Islington, a new church designated the Church of Humanity and dedicated to a somewhat novel religion known as Logical Positivism.

This religion was based on the materialistic philosophy of Auguste Comte, a curious man who, having failed in an attempt to drown himself in the Seine and wearied John Stuart Mill and Sir William Molesworth with his clamant and persistent demands for money, succumbed to cancer in 1857.

In some respects the Positivist creed approximated to the Nietzschean concept of superman, but, less aristocratic, it dethroned the gods of current belief and set up the welfare of mankind as object of worship in their place. Discounting the first stage of the human mind (religious beliefs), ignoring the second (metaphysical ideals), it concentrated its attentions upon what it regarded as the third and highest stage (the positivist), and sought, by means of a reassessment of social and moral values in the light of the exact sciences, to reconstruct the fabric of society and foster a perfect social harmony. Just how it proposed to do this seems a little vague, but outside the Falkland Street church was blazoned the invincible trinity of Positivist dicta:

> "Love for Principle
> Order for Basis
> Progress for Aim."

The evangel in Liverpool owed its beginnings to a Dr. Richard Carson and a Mr. Albert Crompton, the son of Judge Crompton and a prominent member of a big Liverpool shipping firm. On the death of Carson, the apostolate devolved upon Albert Crompton who held office until his death in Paris in 1904. He was succeeded by Mr. Sydney Style, a Liverpool solicitor, who lived at number 69 Hope Street.

Bald, acquiline and bearded, Mr. Style fulfilled the position of leader of the sect with distinction, not only presiding at the Sunday evening devotional meetings at Falkland Street, but also throwing his own home open for social soirées every Thursday night.

By 1913, thirty years after its foundation, the Positivist Society, its members now about 150 strong, was quietly flourishing. Many of the congregation were people of substance, and work was almost complete on a fine new church which had been built, close to Mr. Style's home, on the Upper Parliament Street corner of Hope Street. Embellished with a large statue of the Society's symbolic mother and child, it was to replace the old church in Falkland Street, and was to be known as the Temple of Humanity. During the three decades of their existence, the Positivists might not have made any spectacular contribution to the welfare of mankind in Liverpool, but at least they had done no harm, and one cannot but feel that fate was needlessly cruel when, towards the end of that year, it dealt to that innocent company of eccentrics a blow from which it was never really to recover.

It was in the unlikely person of an illiterate, 23-year-old journeyman-joiner, William M'Donald, that the unsuspecting Positivists met their downfall.

M'Donald, whose family lived in Rishton Street, Everton, was an almost fanatic adherent of dialectical materialism. A keen socialist in the militant tradition of Shaw, Wells and Mr. Keir Hardie, it was only to be expected that he would subscribe wholeheartedly to any philosophy that preached the establishment of socialism on a scientific basis as a religion. Although never a member of the Positivist congregation, M'Donald had, since he was eighteen, attended educational evening-classes organised by the Church of Humanity, and was a frequent visitor at Mr. and Mrs. Style's Thursday evening soirées. A shabby undistinguished figure, whose wisp of beard betrayed the fact that he had never shaved, M'Donald seemed curiously out of place in the big L-shaped room with its tinkling grand-piano and liberal buffet. He moved freely among the guests, the perpetual, self-complacent smile on his lips belying the real unease of his heart, but always his restless eyes searched for Miss Crompton.

Mary Crompton, a 42-year-old spinster, was the daughter of that Albert Crompton who had preceded Mr. Style as Positivist prophet-in-chief. She was, in consequence, an important member of the Society, and she had shown many, quite impersonal, little kindnesses to the gauche M'Donald. She seems, indeed, to have been an exceptionally kindly woman, for at least two other members of that small circle had reason to be grateful to her goodness of heart.

One of these was a young man named Richard Price Roberts. He was by trade a copper engraver and he was a member of the Church of Humanity.

Actually, it was he who first introduced M'Donald to the Positivists, having made his acquaintance at a socialist meeting near St. George's Hall.

The other was 24-year-old Paul Gaze who, having been left an orphan at an early age, was adopted (though not legally) by Miss Crompton, who made herself responsible for his education, welfare and upbringing. As he grew older, Gaze formed an ardent attachment for his benefactress. She, bewildered and somewhat overcome by it all, did everything in her power to discourage his attentions, and eventually he went as the representative of a London chemical-manufacturing firm to Brazil. There, he met and fell in love with a young Brazilian girl and, much relieved, Miss Crompton, who was an accomplished linguist and spoke Portuguese fluently, went to Brazil and brought the young couple back to Liverpool to be married.

William M'Donald, Richard Price Roberts, Paul Gaze and Mary Crompton—those are the *dramatis personae*.

Sydney Style's hospitable home in Hope Street and the rising edifice of the Temple of Humanity—that is the back-cloth.

The stage is set.

The actors are assembled.

Now is the time for the curtain-rise—and fall.

Shortly after 9-30 p.m. on the evening of Tuesday, October 7th, 1913, William M'Donald rang the bell at 142 Islington, the house where Richard Price Roberts lodged. In his pocket was a fully-charged, five-chambered revolver, several loose cartridges and a razor. In his hand, a stout, foot-long cane, tipped with a heavy iron knob. When Roberts opened the door, M'Donald dealt him a vicious blow on the head with the cane, drew forth the revolver and fired two shots at him. Somewhat stunned, but otherwise uninjured, the terrified Roberts made a bolt for his bedroom. M'Donald made no attempt to follow him, but ran off into the night.

From there M'Donald made his way to Grove Street where he met Paul gaze. He accompanied him to his lodgings at number 62. The pair went into the front room together. At about 10-15 p.m. the servant-girl, Elizabeth Taylor, heard two revolver shots, followed by the sounds of M'Donald's hurried departure. Trembling, she pushed open the parlour door. Gaze was lying in the fireplace. He was quite dead. He had been shot through the temple. A second bullet was lodged in his arm.

Meanwhile, M'Donald was knocking at the door of number 81 Bedford Street South—Miss Crompton's home. Miss Crompton had retired upstairs, but M'Donald told the maid that he wanted to see her on a matter of the utmost urgency. "I suppose I must go down," said Miss Crompton wearily to Miss Huckwell, who had been her companion for twenty-seven years.

M'Donald was waiting in the sitting-room. As soon as Miss Crompton entered he shot her through the temple. Then he turned the gun on himself. Detectives found Miss Crompton lying on the sitting-room floor. Directly opposite her, also on the floor, was M'Donald. He, too, had a bullet wound in his temple, but he was not dead. He was rushed to the Royal Infirmary, but he died at 2-30 the following morning without recovering consciousness.

★ ★ ★ ★

Oddly enough, it is to the first tenet of Positivism that we must turn for an explanation of that long-ago night of tragedy—"Love for Principle."

Poor, half-educated William M'Donald had fallen violently in love with Miss Crompton. In the words of one who knew her, "It was impossible to imagine anyone less like *une femme fatale* than she was, but that was the part she was called upon to play at the fall of the curtain. A lady of uncertain age, she was in no way beautiful—just faded and weary. Her clothes were undeniably expensive, but lacked chic. The wonder of it is that this marcescent spinster, who looked older than her years, should have inspired passion in the breasts of two youths"—one of whom cared so much that he killed her.

All the evidence clearly establishes that there was nothing whatsoever between Miss Crompton and M'Donald. They met alone only once—on the night of her death. True, on one occasion she did call at his home—he was ill and she came to make kindly inquiries of his family. Indeed, it was probably because she seemed unmoved by his attentions that M'Donald shot her, and there is no doubt that he murdered the unfortunate Gaze in a fit of jealousy because of his resentment of his relationship with her. Roberts, too, was closely associated with Miss Crompton, and for no other reason M'Donald attempted to kill him.

The circumstances of Gaze's death were particularly tragic, for he had just returned with his Brazilian bride from his honeymoon. It was a strict rule of the Positivist creed that newly-married couples should sleep apart and meet only for meals during the first three months of their marriage. Gaze was killed before those three months had elapsed so the marriage was never consummated.

The Church of Humanity never really recovered from the effects of this terrible scandal, although it struggled on for another quarter of a century.

Mr. and Mrs. Style could still be seen walking, rather forlornly, from their house to the nearby Temple. On Sunday 8 Shakespeare 74 (16th September, 1928), they celebrated their golden wedding there, and the Sacrament of Presentation was conferred upon their grandson, David Sydney Ellis. But it was almost the last flicker of a dying fire.

Presently there was only Mr. Style, more bent, his beard now snowy-white. Then he was seen in Hope Street no more, and his place was taken by a German, Otto Baier. But his ministry was short-lived and he preached to empty pews.

In 1941 a club for Norwegian seamen was established in the basement of the whilom Temple.

Finally, on October 19th, 1947, the old building was rededicated to become the Third Church of Christ Scientist. The statue was removed. The last trace of the Positivists had faded away.

Now there is nothing—nothing except that empty alcove twenty or so feet up on the red brick face of an unobtrusive church on the darker side of Upper Parliament Street . . .

15. OF AUTUMN, POLTERGEISTS AND PARSONAGES

The long quiet dusk of the year is gathering. Night hides behind a veil of mist, and late afternoon is wreathed in the acrid smoke of burning leaves. There is upon the air the slightest whisper of frost that flees the mind to inglenooks and glowing fires, to short dark days and cosy Pickwickian nights.

After the promise of spring and the fulfilment of summer, autumn comes as a period of brief fruition, but heavily charged with ominous portents of winter's long stagnation. Everywhere is a faint suggestion of urgency; an atmosphere of hurried preparation. It is as if all nature is preparing to withstand a siege. Nor is man entirely dispensed from the necessity of making everything ready. The city dweller, perhaps, need not be deeply concerned. Winter is for him a mere matter of increased electrification. But for the countryman it is often a desperate race against the great white legions that rush down upon him from the North. It is a race also against the expanding frontiers of darkness, and in many a country village in the past the rank smell of molten tallow, betokening the dipping of the frames of winter candles, was as much a hall-mark of autumn as the odour of burning weeds. For the wild things, it is the season when they must hasten to hide. The dormouse, fat and sleek from feasts of rich brown cobnuts, curls up within his winter nest, and the hedgehog, replete and plump, lies, a snoring ball of prickles, snugly bedded in his leaf-lined hibernaculum beneath the hedgerow roots. It is a time of death or death-like sleep. The mind, tired as the body, perceives in silhouettes. It hovers about dreams. Dreams at which we might laugh in summertide's high noon, but which will become nightmares as the twilight enters our very bones. And, as the short sharp gusts of autumn gales rattle the casements, and the wind sobs and mews about the corners of the house, plucking the shrivelled foliage from tall trees where the black shapes of rooks make melancholy circles against a ragged sky, we draw closer to the spurting fire as though to find refuge in its warmth and light from the darkness and the legacy of fear it bears from the superstitious childhood of mankind.

Suddenly and silently the night is upon us, and the cottage windows are glimmering glow-worm points. But we will linger a while in the dusk.

★ ★ ★ ★

Now is the time when the poltergeist enters into its own. Unseen, unheard, if not unsensed, it has lurked long behind the thin screen of its invisibility. It is nourished by the ebb-tide of nature and resistance. Scepticism has seeped away with the fading daylight.

Before us the parsonage stands bleak and black amidst trees which sprang and grew within its shade and now stretch gnarled protection over it. It is empty—deserted; yet should the dead eyes of its windows reflect white, waving images we shall feel no surprise. We know its history. Here, man fought a losing battle against an amorphous adversary. It is all well-documented and has been meticulously and continuously investigated. But, the reason asks, how are these shades possible? Have we not said that the parsonage is without its parson? It is dark and empty of people. The orchard where vicarage children laughed is dripping and deserted. Autumn blooms of dead-nettle are in the place of the dahlias. That black glassless gap on the left of the conservatory's white-painted skeleton was once the study, where with books and buttered toast, with fragrant China tea and cheery chintz and brass to multiply and mirror dancing fire-flames, the vicar waged his war against the unseen forces which gathered like drudging autumn clouds about his vicarage. Here, night after night, he sat and heard the brittle whisperings of dry leaves cease as rain began to fall, and the sudden squalls of equinoctial gales drove it tapping like goblin fingers against the window-pane. Here, the alerted senses seized upon the startled scamper of a mouse behind the wainscot, the creakings of an old staircase, the fancied sound of movement whence no movement should have come. So did these things blend into a subtle symphony of fear played on the taut strings of nerves. On and on to the crescendo, the climacteric of terror, to die away in the shudder which sprang not from the draught where the wind crept through the small crack in the wooden window-frame, but out of vague imaginings and formless apprehensions.

And later, from the illusory safety of his feather-bed in the flower-papered room that smelt of clean linen, moth-balls and the comforting fumes of the paraffin stove, the vicar would listen to the peals of bells, the clatter of smashed crockery and the demonic laughter that echoed through the sleeping house until his wife's trembling set the brass knobs rattling on the bedposts.

At last the parsonage was abandoned, and the triumphant frenzies of the poltergeist filled only empty rooms.

Perhaps, like Borley Rectory, it will all end in smoke. Some poltergeist inclined to incendiarism will strike the phantom flints and the parsonage will become their blazing tinder. One autumn evening, maybe, there will be a red glow in the sky and the smoke from the funeral-pyre of a dead legend will mingle with the fumes of damply-smouldering weeds, and, rising, will drift away in dark clouds to gather again, perhaps, about some other parsonage upon a distant autumn evening.